OXFORD

Felix Markham

Oxford

Introduction by C. M. Bowra
Photographs by Penny Tweedie
Notes on Illustrations by Ian Lowe

Mowbrays
London & Oxford

First published 1967 by George Weidenfeld and Nicolson Ltd
This edition first published 1975 by A. R. Mowbray and Co. Ltd
The Alden Press, Osney Mead, Oxford OX2 OEG

ISBN 0 264 66319 5

Printed in Great Britain by
Lowe & Brydone (Printers) Ltd, Thetford, Norfolk

Contents

Introduction

The right time to visit Oxford was 1850. Its medieval and classical buildings were still unspoiled and unrestored, and the latest addition to them, the Ashmolean Museum, which had just been completed, was worthy of a place in their company. The visitor walked straight from fields or market-gardens into the old town, over bridges from east, south and west, or into the spacious street of St Giles from the north. The dominating stone façades of the colleges were interspersed with timbered or plastered houses, and at the end of almost every street was a church. All this was soon changed. When dons were allowed to marry, the solid Gothic fantasies of north Oxford rose to meet their philoprogenitive needs. Already in 1879 Gerard Manley Hopkins, who praised the city for its intimate intermingling with natural things, lamented its 'base and brickish skirt', though by modern standards he had little to complain of. Today the Oxford of 1850 is embedded in a sprawl of modern developments which swamp the countryside and seep into the heart of the medieval city. The literary pilgrim, who wishes to walk in the footsteps of the Scholar Gipsy or Jude the Obscure, of Verdant Green or Zuleika Dobson, will find his tracks obstructed by garages, chain-stores, and laboratories. On what were once the tennis- and croquet-lawns of the University Parks natural science has with a bold inventiveness of styles erected massive temples to its imperial spirit. Anyone who wishes to discover the traditional Oxford has to face disappointments, but in the end he will find it behind the traffic-jams and the serried lines of parked cars, still spacious with its quadrangles and its gardens, still refusing to admit the passage of years.

This mixture of past and present is reflected in Oxford institutions. Ancient habits, which have lost their first meaning, are refurbished to serve new purposes. The college system, which passed out of use in Paris in the Middle Ages, still dominates the life of Oxford. Colleges still provide, as they always have, board and lodging but also much more. They were once intended to look after the whole well-being, physical, moral, and intellectual, of their charges, and these intentions still survive actively in the provision of academic instruction. So complete and so conscientious is the teaching provided by college tutors that public lectures, organised by the University, are of secondary importance, if only because attendance at them is not enforced by threats and penalties as it is with a private hour. Colleges vie with one another to get good results in examinations, and local journals construct curious league-tables to illustrate the incidence of first, second, third, and fourth classes. The tutorial system is a vigorous survival from the medieval system of 'reading with a master', and keeps many of its virtues. Though the teacher is still expected to guide his pupils with the utmost care in their studies, he has less control in other matters. Not very long ago colleges expected undergraduates to conform to a

1 Vaulting over the choir of the Cathedral (late 15th century). Christ Church

complex code of rules and imposed punishments for any breach of them. Of course some rules are necessary for any community of young people living in close proximity to one another, but it is easy to be too ingenious in devising rules for almost every emergency, and this the colleges did, only to find that most of them were broken. So also for centuries the colleges followed the national example in trying to brainwash everyone in matters of theology, and in due course this also failed. Two world wars discredited most of the more foolish rules, but colleges still feel responsible for their undergraduates in such matters as health and finance and are very far from sharing the continental indifference to what the young do or suffer, while for their part the young, who pride themselves on their self-sufficiency, turn in time of trouble to their colleges for help.

In its first centuries Oxford was a democratic society. Since its main task was to train men for service in the church and so for the state, which drew its officials from the class of clerics, it supported with scholarship those whom it thought fitted for such duties. As the scope of the clergy decreased and laymen became more literate and more eager to administer the realm, rich young men were sent to Oxford as a preliminary to public life, and it was they who set its tone from the beginning of the seventeenth century to the first quarter of the twentieth. Before 1914 poorer scholars could still manage to get through on their scholarships, and apart from a few 'bloods' on one side and a few sots on the other, members of colleges usually managed to keep on tolerant terms with one another, if only because they were members of a single community and took part in its common activities. But even before 1914 it was clear that entry to Oxford lay not through examination-tests, which were shamefully easy, but in the ability to pay fees. This was even more the case between the two wars, when for financial reasons colleges accepted a number of candidates whose intellectual claims were painfully slender. What saved and transformed Oxford was the Butler Act of 1944. But for it Oxford could hardly have continued to exist; for fees were now too high for the old clientele. By securing that the state financed all who were able to profit by a university education, the Act entirely altered the character of Oxford and demolished the all too justifiable charge that it admitted only the rich. The enormous social changes which followed coincided with vast other social changes after the second war, and largely for this reason took place without any noticeable tension. Oxford, rather unfairly known as the 'home of lost causes', was this time on the winning side, but made no fuss about it.

Though undergraduates pride themselves on their independence of spirit, their habits of thinking cannot fail to be conditioned by the intellectual discipline to which they are subjected. In Oxford the mere collection of facts has never been thought to be enough; still less is there any tendency to believe that all facts are equal before the throne. What counts most is the ability to think, to detect false arguments and bad evidence, to construct a coherent case, to see more than one side of a matter and to decide which is best, to make words perform their task with the utmost clarity and precision. This, which seems so modern, is a heritage from the middle ages, from the training in disputation which was given by the schoolmen from the twelfth century and which was still vigorous and exacting in the early part of the nineteenth when it influenced such masters of intricate argument as J. H. Newman and W. E. Gladstone. So powerful has this influence been that it may even explain why Oxford has produced far fewer good poets than Cambridge. It is true that in the nineteenth century the single college of Balliol nursed Swinburne, Clough, Arnold, and Hopkins, but this is a glittering exception. On the other hand, though at Oxford the taste for words may be severely drilled, at times it bursts into a noble art of expression in the hands of such masters as Walter Raleigh, Thomas

2 *The Adoration of the Magi;* detail of the tapestry (1890) by Sir Edward
Burne-Jones and William Morris. Exeter College Chapel

Browne, Hobbes, Samuel Johnson, de Quincey, Ruskin, and Pater. Yet, though universities rightly take pride in their men of genius in the arts, they have little to offer them in the way of help. By expelling Shelley for writing a tract on the necessity of atheism, Oxford did him a good turn, for it allowed his creative gifts to develop without any restricting discipline.

The cult of strict analytical argument from first principles has at intervals won Oxford a name for being hostile to new spheres of knowledge. In the not too distant past it has in turn opposed the full recognition of economics, anthropology, psychology, and sociology, and though it has yielded on all of these, much to its own benefit, it will no doubt resist other proposals for courses which seem not to satisfy its standards of discipline and method. Its attitude towards science shows how wayward its movements can be. In the thirteenth century Roger Bacon embodied the new spirit of scientific enquiry and was not at all afraid of controversy. In the seventeenth century Oxford was one of the birthplaces of the Royal Society. Even in the eighteenth century it threw up an occasional physician or astronomer. But in the nineteenth century, when science was really born again, Oxford was slow to see what was happening and missed resplendent chances of leading the world. It had indeed its grand moments as when in the new Science Museum T.H.Huxley and Bishop Samuel Wilberforce debated on the descent of man, but its preoccupation with theology and logic caused it to lag behind Cambridge and London. The reputation thus gained still persists, though for the last fifty years Oxford has made prodigious efforts to win a proper place in the scientific world. It has now the largest schools of chemistry and physics in the country, and in quite recent years three Presidents of the Royal Society have been Oxford professors, each of whom has won a Nobel Prize and been awarded the Order of Merit.

The relation of tutor and pupil is based on the assumption that the good tutor is also a scholar and researcher, whose own desire to master a certain branch of knowledge will convey to his pupils some of the dignity and the excitement of intellectual enquiry. To maintain the balance between research and teaching is never easy, and too often one may be sacrificed to the other. There are of course excellent teachers who feel no call to do research, and there are excellent researchers who think that teaching merely interferes with their proper work. Yet on the whole research is as much respected at Oxford as at most other universities, and though it is seldom measured by its quantity, any successful exhibition of it calls for praise. It may be done in almost any subject, from the widest and most familiar to the most recondite and most esoteric. Some of it may seem to be of little use when it appears, and then later it is found to make an indispensable contribution to some wide discovery; much of it, however exciting at first, may be discredited by later work and soon be forgotten. Yet with all its uncertainties and failures the pursuit of knowledge plays a large part in Oxford. In natural science it proceeds over a broad front in an unceasing series of small operations; in the humanities it varies from an intricate examination of some detail to bold projects which demand years for their completion. Since a university is judged outside largely by the books that issue from it, the reputation of Oxford certainly owes much to generations in which the tradition of learning has been cultivated over many fields and brought its scholars and scientists into touch with their fellows elsewhere. It is this pursuit of knowledge which gives Oxford a place of dignity among other places of learning and strengthens it in its belief in itself. This is the centre from which much else radiates – the high level of teaching, the willingness to discuss many matters carefully and seriously, the ambition to write good books and thereby to set an example of what learning really means to those who pursue it.

In origin the colleges were monastic institutions, and such in some important respects they remain. Though women are now full members of the university, they are in a minority of one to seven, and though they mix as freely with young men as in any American or continental university, they inevitably miss much in a system that was built for men only. Even this degree of tolerance has been secured only after long struggles. When the first college for women was founded at Oxford in 1878, they were kept almost in purdah and supervised even at university lectures by chaperones of forbidding aspect. Between the wars fierce and lamentably successful efforts were made to restrict their numbers, and behind much argument lurked a fear that their presence might somehow make the young men less manly. The second war swept away the last restrictions on women, but they had by now formed their own kind of college life, and it was not easy to escape from this or from the pattern which it imposed on their habits.

Nearly all undergraduates live for their first year in college and a large proportion of them for their second year. After this they retire into lodgings, which may be at some distance from their colleges and make it easier for them to work for their final examinations without distraction. Their years in college mould their personalities and enable them to break the boundaries set by home and school. From a wide selection of human types they can choose those with whom they have most in common, but they also come into contact with others whose backgrounds are quite unfamiliar and stretch their minds in new directions. They are free to be as absurd as they like and to indulge the paradoxes and poses which were frowned upon at school. In this way they can work them out of their systems just as by laughter and satire they can surmount their dislike of habits and points of view which seem to them barbarous. Talk at all levels is the life-blood of undergraduates. Through it they find unlimited enjoyment and incidentally clear their minds on many perplexing matters. Nor does it matter if what they say is of no importance. It helps them to face the world and to be not too discouraged by its prospects.

Both dons and students at Oxford live in circumstances of considerable charm and even beauty. The ancient buildings catch the eye and the imagination, and the gardens, concealed behind gray stone walls, keep the peace of a less bustling age. It is true that modernity, in the form of plumbing, has been slow to assert itself in the colleges and that till quite recently Rhodes scholars from the Commonwealth or the United States complained that they could not get a bath without crossing a quadrangle, while even dons lived in what was regarded as luxurious squalor. These little anachronisms have been mended, and Oxford is now criticised for being too comfortable. In this a slight touch of envy may perhaps enforce righteous indignation at the size of some dwelling-rooms, formal dinners in college halls, luxuriously stocked flower beds, immaculately kept lawns, and ample playing-fields. Why should these anomalies not be replaced by bed-sitting-rooms and cafeterias? The simple answer is that it would cost millions to do so, and that, if it were done, nothing would be gained and a lot would be lost. The so-called luxuries of Oxford are a heritage from more generous ages, which still catch the eye in panelled rooms, or well-stocked libraries, or silver beer-tankards, or good music at religious services. These are creations of an aristocratic society, but they have been placed at the service of all who belong to the democratic society of Oxford. Much of this is not 'really necessary', but that after all is true of almost everything that is worth having. We need not complain, we may even be grateful, that on ceremonial occasions speeches are still made in Latin, that in procession the Vice-Chancellor is preceded by four bedels with silver staves, that gowns are worn at lectures and examinations, that on May Day at dawn choristers sing on the top of Magdalen Tower. These are survivals from the past, but they enliven the present by giving it colour and variety.

Connoisseurs of the English climate claim that Oxford provides a notably bad example of it, with its damp miasma spreading from encircling rivers, its mists and fogs even in July, its thick, clammy days when the walls sweat and any movement is an effort. Yet there are compensations. At sudden capricious moments amends are made for many shortcomings. There are days in spring when all the flowering shrubs and trees seem to break into life together and clothe even north Oxford in a riot of blossom; on winter afternoons the sun, shooting its level beams over roofs and gables, brings out half-hidden colours in the stone; the rich, thick air of summer is tempered by the huge trees, beeches and elms and chestnuts, which spread their shadows on the lawns; swans float on the Isis and Cherwell or rise suddenly on clangorous wings into the air; a rich, pullulating nature compels attention and finds a response in the awakening thoughts of young people.

Undergraduates at Oxford belong to a college which is larger than a large family, more sociable and more tolerant than a school, less bewildering and less amorphous than a university. It is his college, rather than his university, which wins a man's loyalty and provides him with a setting for his three or four years at Oxford. In its accumulated experience it can help him to choose a career. For many centuries Oxford produced a large number of men who actually governed the country, whether in parliament or the civil service or the church or the learned professions, and in the nineteenth century to these were added the burdens of administering territories overseas. Much of this has vanished, but industry and commerce now claim those who would have gone into imperial administration, and the number of Oxford men in the government and higher reaches of the civil service indicates that they are still in the seats of power, and their presence in all political parties is a tribute to the adaptability of their training. The past may still be potent in Oxford, but it does not hamper growth, and we may draw the lesson that through many vicissitudes Oxford has learned to adapt itself to new conditions and to master them in its own way. It has recently shown that it is not afraid to examine its own defects, while the pressure of competition from new up-and-coming universities can do Oxford nothing but good. Oxford has survived for many reasons, but the most reputable of them is that it has maintained the cause of reason and argument, and so long as it continues to rely upon these as its source of energy and inspiration, it will continue to exert its influence.

3

4

5

3   Bishop Fox's standing salt (late 15th century).
    Corpus Christi College
4   'Founder's cup' and mazer (15th century).
    Oriel College

5   Rock crystal salt (1549). Trinity College

6   *(overleaf)* Great Quadrangle to the north-east
    (15th century). Magdalen College

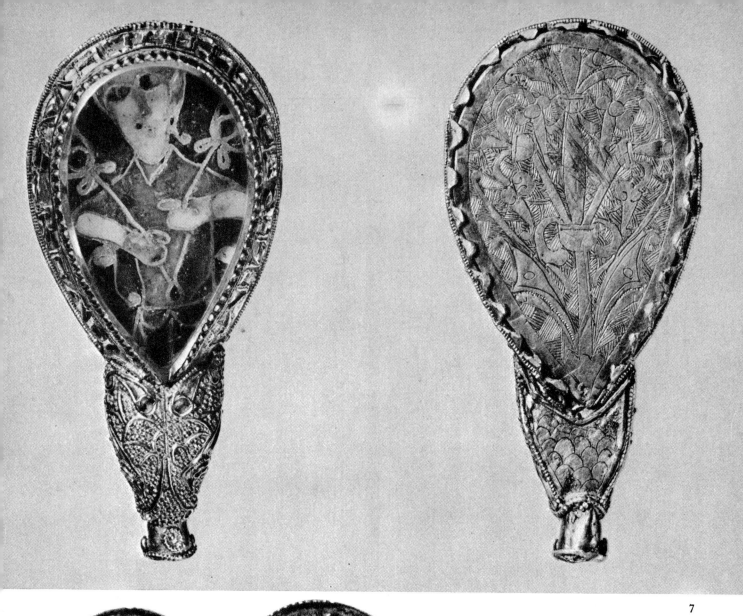

7   The Alfred Jewel (*c.* 890), front and back.
Ashmolean Museum

8   Silver pennies of Aethelred II *(top)* and William I
(bottom), minted in Oxford. Heberden Coin Room,
Ashmolean Museum

1 Medieval Origins

The idea of a university is now so familiar and so taken for granted that we rarely bother to ask what is the meaning of the term, or the origin of the thing itself. It is a specifically medieval invention, handed on, like the jury system and parliament, to the modern world.

The rise of universities begins in that astonishing twelfth century, which has been fairly called a renaissance, comparable in importance and vitality with the great fifth century of Greek civilisation. The origins of the University of Oxford can only be understood in the context of the European order of Christendom, to which it belonged. The adolescent European peoples were awakening after the nightmare of the dark ages which followed the age of Charlemagne and were taking the first steps in the path which was to lead to four centuries of dominance of the West over the East. Their thirst for knowledge and adventure was manifested in the Crusades, the monastic revival, and in the emergence of universities – made possible by the revival of town-life. Nor were these activities contradictory. Increased contact with Byzantine and Islamic civilisation brought the rediscovery of the corpus of Aristotelian philosophy, which provided a mounting intellectual excitement and speculation.

In this first age of medieval civilisation there was a naïve and noble optimism that faith and reason could not clash, which allowed and encouraged the most daring intellectual speculation. It is expressed in the sculptures of Chartres Cathedral, where Plato and Aristotle sit comfortably among the Fathers of the Church, and in the thrusting spire of the University Church of St Mary the Virgin at Oxford. Although all university students were necessarily in minor orders, because in that age all literate professions were the province of the Church, the aim and *raison d'être* of the universities, as distinct from that of the monasteries, was the pursuit of knowledge. Remarkable leniency was shown by the Church to the most startling ideas in the universities, except when it came to open heresy, as in the case of Wyclif, and even he was not molested when his ideas had been formally condemned. As Haskins has pointed out: 'The religious education of a bygone Oxford was an inheritance not from the Middle Ages but from the Reformation.' At the height of the struggle in the nineteenth century to end the control of Oxford by the Anglican Church, Goldwin Smith pertinently noted that 'If we inquire to which of the two antagonistic elements of the medieval intellect the Universities belonged, to that which was sacerdotal and reactionary or to that which was scientific and progressive, we shall find the Universities were the very centre of science and progress; to the sacerdotal and reactionary party, they were the objects of deserved suspicion.'

The pursuit of knowledge followed a pattern of evolution. In the dark ages it was kept alive by the monasteries: in the abortive Carolingian renaissance Charlemagne had ordained that every cathedral should develop a school. In the first half of the twelfth century the cathedral schools began to revive and take over the leadership from the monasteries: Chartres was the shining example. In the second half of the twelfth century the torch passed to the universities, and among universities the lead steadily shifted from south to north, starting with Salerno and Bologna, then Paris, Oxford, Cambridge and Cologne. In medieval parlance a *universitas* meant simply a gild or trade union; hence there were gilds of scholars combining to protect their interests. A university in the modern sense emerged when it became a *studium generale*, a centre of learning of general resort and reputation. No doubt these institutions owed something to the models of the Greco-Roman academies and the Islamic universities: but what entitles the historian to treat them as something novel and revolutionary is the fact that they were permanent, self-governing, numerous and supra-national. Europe was developing a constellation of universities, with an interchangeable population of scholars stimulating and enriching each other. In the early days when universities owned no buildings or property, migration was easy and frequent, and was an effective weapon against oppression by the towns which lodged and fed the scholars. In 1229 King Henry III, in a blatant but unsuccessful attempt to promote a 'brain-drain', wrote a letter inviting the University of Paris to settle in England. There was, in fact, a partial migration in that year to Oxford from Paris, where the University was quarrelling with the Chancellor and the King.

The University of Paris grew directly out of the cathedral school of Nôtre Dame: by the middle of the twelfth century the great teacher Abelard had established its reputation, and students were crowding into the *quartier latin* on the left bank of the Seine. In 1200 King Philip Augustus guaranteed to students trial before an ecclesiastical judge, and in 1215 the papal legate recognised the right of the University to make its own statutes. The University was gradually winning its independence from the Chancellor of the Cathedral.

THE BEGINNINGS OF OXFORD UNIVERSITY

An ordinance of a papal legate in 1214 is the first formal evidence of the development of a university at Oxford. But there is clear evidence that in the course of the twelfth century a *studium generale* had been developing at Oxford. Famous scholars such as Theobald of Étampes, Robert Pullen and Vacarius the Lombard jurist were teaching at Oxford in the first half of the twelfth century. About 1186 Gerald of Wales visited Oxford to lecture, 'because more clerks were to be found there and they more clerkly than elsewhere'. Rashdall confidently asserted that the establishment of a *studium generale* at Oxford could be pinpointed to a migration from Paris in the year 1167, when, during the quarrel between Henry II and Becket, the French king expelled foreign students from Paris, and Henry II ordered English clerks back from Paris. But the great historian of Oxford, Salter, concluded that 'for the theory of a migration there is really no evidence'.

Still less is there any evidence of the legend dating from the reign of Edward III that the University was founded by King Alfred. University College claimed King Alfred as their founder, and in 1727 obtained a judgment from the Court of King's Bench (which is still presumably legally valid) that the foundation of the college by King Alfred was recognised by English law. Cambridge, not to be outdone, produced a charter which proved the foundation of Cambridge to be the work of King Arthur.

We must accept the fact that the university at Oxford just grew, but it remains to be asked why the first *studium generale* in England should have appeared at Oxford. It was clearly an important town long before the university appeared. With some exaggeration the historian J.R. Green pointed out that 'the University of Oxford is so far from being older than the City that Oxford had already seen five centuries of borough life before a student appeared within its streets'. Oxford was Saxon, not Roman, in origin, and it is first mentioned in 912. Its river-crossings (hence Oxen-ford) would make it an important frontier position between the Saxon kingdoms of Wessex and Mercia and would later give it commercial importance. The strict grid-iron plan of the streets of the old city suggest that royal policy turned a manor into a building-site. In the late tenth and early eleventh centuries it was a target for the Danes and was burnt no less than four times. It was also the scene of several important royal witans. William the Conqueror assigned Oxford to one of his barons, Robert D'Oily, who began to build a new Castle. Robert's son founded the great Abbey of Oseney in 1129. When Dr Johnson visited its solitary ruins surviving from the dissolution of the monasteries, he exclaimed 'Sir, to look upon them fills me with indignation'. There was already the Priory of St Frideswide, later absorbed into Christ Church. To the north was the Jewry, where a wealthy community of Jews flourished under royal protection until the banishment of the Jews in 1289.

Under the two D'Oilys Oxford rapidly recovered, and in 1130 its aid to the king ranked ninth in size in the whole kingdom. It shared only with London and Winchester the right to assist the king's butler at the coronation. Oxford was highly favoured by the Norman and Angevin kings, Henry I and Henry II. Both were literate and intellectual monarchs who relished the conversation of the clerks of Oxford. The royal palace of Beaumont was built by Henry I outside the North Gate (hence Beaumont Street), and his hunting lodge was built at Woodstock, where he kept his zoo. Richard Coeur de Lion, son of Henry II and Eleanor of Aquitaine, was born at Beaumont Palace. In 1155 Henry II confirmed by charter to his 'citizens of Oxenford' the privileges, especially their 'gild-merchant' granted by Henry I, and 'all other customs and liberties and laws of their own which they have in common with my citizens of London'. The combination of geographical situation, commercial prosperity, monastic splendour, and royal favour is probably enough to account for Oxford as the setting for the growth of a *studium generale*. It is significant that about 1180 a conveyance records that illuminators, parchmenters and a book-binder were settled in 'Cattestrete' close by St Mary's Church.

In 1209 the citizens of Oxford, with the encouragement of King John, hanged some students for an alleged murder, and the university dispersed to Paris and elsewhere, including Cambridge. As Rashdall remarks in his *Medieval Universities of Europe in the Middle Ages*, 'what attracted them to that distant marsh town we do not know'; but this migration helped to develop a new *studium generale* at Cambridge. In 1214 the citizens of Oxford made their peace with the Oxford scholars through the papal legate, whose ordinance laid down that any clerk arrested by the townsmen should be surrendered on the demand of the Bishop of Lincoln, or the archdeacon or his official, or the Chancellor 'whom the Bishop shall set over the scholars'. Oxford was later threatened by two partial migrations, which proved to be temporary. In 1264, during the Barons' War, some students migrated to Northampton but were induced to return after the victory of the King. In 1334 a violent riot between the Northern and Southern students at Oxford led to a partial migration to Stamford. As late as 1827 all candidates for an Oxford degree had to take an oath not to give or attend lectures at Stamford.

The historian Matthew Paris records that three thousand scholars left Oxford in the migration of 1209. Fifteen hundred is a more likely figure, but even this number of students, who might range in age from fourteen to forty, would create formidable problems in a city of the size of Oxford. Haskins remarks that 'the violence of medieval university life was almost equalled by its bibulosity'.

Medieval letters from students have survived mainly in the form of stock letters composed by professional letter-writers. A specimen from Oxford shows the perennial preoccupation of the student: 'B to his Venerable Master A. Greetings. This is to inform you that I am studying at Oxford with the greatest diligence, but the matter of money stands greatly in the way of my promotion, as it is now two months since I spent the last of what you sent me. The city is expensive and makes many demands; I have to rent lodgings, buy necessaries, and provide for many other things which I cannot now specify. Wherefore I respectfully beg your paternity that by the promptings of divine pity you may assist me and that I may be able to complete what I have begun. For you must know that without Ceres and Bacchus Apollo grows cold.' Even more topical is the situation faced by a medieval parent in Besançon who writes to his son, 'I have recently discovered that you live dissolutely and slothfully, preferring license to restraint, and strumming a guitar while the others are at their studies.'

The University as yet had no property, buildings or endowments: it is still nearly a century before the foundation of the first colleges. The students lived in lodgings or in houses rented by groups of scholars. One of the provisions of the legatine Ordinance of 1214 obliged the citizens to remit half the rents of the hostels and schools occupied by the scholars for the next ten years. The University early secured recognition, with royal backing, of the rule common to the medieval universities of Europe that houses once let to scholars should not revert to laymen. It was a short step for the University to insist that the lessees of these houses or Halls should be Masters of Arts, responsible to the Chancellor as Principals for the rent and the discipline of their boarders. Vagabond scholars who were not enrolled under the discipline of a Master were to be banished from the city or imprisoned. At their peak there were some seventy of these Halls, and centuries were to pass before the colleges generally took over from the Halls responsibility for undergraduates. Throughout the medieval period, the centre of life for the vast majority of undergraduate students was their Hall, the schools where lectures were given, and the tavern. A few Halls were to grow into endowed colleges, such as Brasenose, Pembroke, Worcester and Hertford Colleges; St Edmund Hall was the sole medieval Hall to survive to the present century, and to retain its name when it became a college in 1956.

Oxford University had an easier task than the University of Paris in asserting its independence and self-government because Oxford was not a cathedral city and the episcopal seat at Lincoln was far away; moreover, in the formative period of the first half of the thirteenth century, the Bishop of Lincoln, Robert Grosseteste, had been, before his translation, the foremost Oxford scholar of the day and 'Master of the Schools'. By title and origin the Bishop's official, the Chancellor soon became the nominee of the Congregation of Masters: he thus became their champion and representative, and also transferred the episcopal jurisdiction to the University. His powers grew with each crisis in the chronic struggle with the citizens.

In 1248 we first hear of the two Proctors nominated by the Congregation of Masters, representing the scholars from North and South, assisting the Chancellor in administration and jurisdiction. In 1244 a quarrel with the Jews in Oxford provoked a royal edict giving to the

mu. h̄. eſt equi fluctualeſ. ✠ De BALENA.

Abelua mmaǎ ꝗ̄ cꝛꝛꝼ iſǔ bꝺ ꝺeloꝛꝼ ꝺꝼ L ꝼꝼeꝺ

Chancellor the right to deal with all cases of contract and debt in which students were involved. In 1248 the King ordered every mayor and bailiff on taking office to swear to respect university liberties and customs, and gave the Chancellor and Proctors the right to be present at the assay of bread and ale – a crucial point when the interests of consumers had to be protected against the producers. Friction between town and gown came to a head in a riot in 1298, and much more dramatically and decisively in the three days' battle which started on St Scholastica's Day, 10 February, 1355. Local quarrels were by then aggravated by the popular unrest and anti-clerical feeling following the scourge of the Black Death. A trivial tavern brawl sparked off a general rising of the townsmen, assisted by the peasants. The Chancellor and the scholars fled the town, after defeat and slaughter in street fighting. The King's Commissioners came down heavily on the side of the University. The mayor was imprisoned and two hundred townsmen were arrested. A new charter confirmed and extended the privileges of the University: the town was heavily fined, and it was not till 1825 that the burgesses were released from an annual penance on St Scholastica's Day. Two centuries of contention and strife ended in a conclusive victory for the Chancellor and the University.

ROYAL AND PAPAL PROTECTION

Why, we may well ask, did kings and popes show such favour to the young university? Their motives were a mixture of idealism and utility. From the practical point of view, the huge administration of the Church needed a supply of literate and trained minds, and they were equally needed by the rapidly growing royal administration. There was the additional attraction that their salaries could be provided out of ecclesiastical benefices and bishoprics. It is significant that more than half the English bishops in the thirteenth century were graduates, and in the fourteenth century the proportion of bishops who were primarily civil servants tended to increase. The bidding prayer recited at Oxford University sermons makes the point concisely: 'that there may never be wanting a succession of persons duly qualified for the service of God in Church and State' and it is a point which recurs, if less concisely, in modern reports on higher education.

King Edward IV wrote in a letter, 'Oxford is the place where the Trivium and Quadrivium [i.e., the seven liberal arts] have laid their foundations, where the fountain of the theological faculty gushes forth, and where the naked souls of the sons of men are clothed with philosophy.' When Henry VIII's courtiers were licking their lips over the prospect of swallowing college as well as monastic endowments, he rapped them sharply on the knuckles. 'I tell you, Sirs, that I judge no land in England better bestowed than that which is given to our Universities. For by their maintenance our Realm shall be well governed when we be dead and rotten.'

In an age of faith, moreover, the possibility of recovering the wisdom of the ancient world and of demonstrating by reason the truths of revelation was a matter of the highest concern; and the theologians were accorded the prestige which in our own age is given to the nuclear and space scientists.

THE COMING OF THE FRIARS

The arrival of the Dominican Friars in Oxford in 1221, and of the Franciscan Friars three years later, greatly enhanced the prestige of the growing university. At the beginning of the thirteenth century two outstanding men of religious genius, Dominic in Languedoc and Francis in

Umbria, were launching movements of startling impact. The mendicant Orders of Dominican Black Friars and Franciscan Grey Friars were to espouse poverty and go to the people. The life and example of St Francis attracted the greatest minds and noblest spirits of the age. Inevitably, the friars became the confessors and advisers of popes, kings, bishops and magnates. The preaching, poverty and enthusiasm of the earliest Franciscans were a marked contrast to the wealth and ease of the older monastic orders. The twin summits of medieval scholastic theology were to be the Franciscan St Bonaventure, the 'Sublime Doctor', and the Dominican St Thomas Aquinas, the 'Angelic Doctor'.

At Oxford especially the interaction between the scholars and the Franciscans was to produce a remarkable flowering. From the start Grosseteste, not only the 'magister scholarum' but also a religious reformer, statesman and organiser, welcomed the Franciscans with enthusiasm, and becoming their first lecturer, turned their attention to learning and divinity. His greatest friend, Adam Marsh, entered the order, and from Grosseteste's initiative sprang the great line of Oxford Franciscan theologians and philosophers – Adam Marsh, Thomas of York, Roger Bacon, Duns Scotus and William of Occam. In fact, with the exception of Bonaventure, all the great Franciscan scholastics were Englishmen.

This development was, paradoxically, far from the intention of St Francis, who was hostile to learning and declared that a great scholar when he joined the order ought to resign even his learning, in order that, having stripped himself of such a possession, he might offer himself naked to the arms of the Crucified. The first leader of the Franciscans in England, Agnellus of Pisa, chosen by St Francis, was perturbed by the impact of Oxford on his flock. 'Woe is me! Simple brothers enter Heaven, while learned brothers dispute whether there be a God at all.' It is ironical that the philosophical ideas and influence of William of Occam, the last of the line, should have done more than anything to disintegrate the medieval synthesis and to promote the rapid decline and sterility of scholasticism.

THE MEDIEVAL QUEST FOR KNOWLEDGE

It is a good deal easier to describe the process than the content of education at the medieval university. To this day the Latin formulae and oaths of the degree ceremony at Oxford preserve the form and terminology of medieval graduation: and the university examinations are still called Public Examinations, from the medieval method of examining by public disputation. The young clerk who entered the university at the age of fourteen or fifteen passed no formal test for admission: there was no university requirement of matriculation until the sixteenth century, and he merely attached himself to a Master. The sole basic course was arts, based on the seven liberal arts, divided into the trivium of grammar, rhetoric, logic and the quadrivium of geometry, arithmetic, astronomy, music. As books were scarce objects, teaching was by classes and lectures, in which texts, predominantly the Latin translations of Aristotle, were dictated and expounded. By his third year the student might be ready to become a 'questionist', taking part in the disputations with the Bachelors. A year later, he could take the examination for the baccalaureate, an entirely oral examination, in the form of further disputation with the Masters, which might last several days. By passing into the ranks of Bachelors, he was said to 'determine' and was licensed by the Chancellor to give the less formal lectures.

Three more years of study, lecturing and disputation would be required before he could supplicate to be admitted or 'incept' as M.A. As an M.A. and a member of Congregation, he was bound to two years of Necessary Regency, lecturing and disputing. The few who survived

this long course could aspire to the higher faculties and doctorates of medicine, law, or theology, and these higher degrees required at least seven years after the M.A. and might take twice as long. Such a rigorous and expensive training made the Doctor a scarce and highly-prized commodity, and if he did not stay in the university he could aspire to valuable place and emolument. Even if the modern historian may be inclined to condemn the intellectual futility of medieval scholasticism, he can hardly deny that this method of education by public disputation, with its emphasis on precision, readiness of mind and lucid communication, was a highly effective form of training for the future civil servant, diplomatist and statesman.

The rise of the medieval universities is associated with a shift of interest from grammar and rhetoric to logic. It was valued not merely as an intellectual training, but as a method of reasoning which must lead to valid and demonstrable conclusions about the nature of reality. Professor David Knowles explains that 'the scholastics of the golden age had the conviction that metaphysical truth and revealed truth were parts of a great whole which the human intellect was capable of harmonising and integrating'. This basic assumption is so remote from the thinking of the modern world that it is impossible to describe, let alone to do justice to medieval scholastic philosophy. One can only refer the reader to the expert historians of ideas whose researches are now revealing the extraordinary richness, complexity and subtlety of medieval thought.

It is easy to see now that so daring and even naïve an aspiration was doomed to failure, and by the time of William of Occam, who convinced many of his contemporaries and followers that the truths of revelation were beyond the reach of reason, disillusion set in. Perhaps the division between theology and philosophy was already foreshadowed in the twelfth century, when St Bernard denounced the daring speculations of Abelard, who himself admitted in the end that 'I would not be an Aristotle if this were to separate me from Christ'. Nevertheless the great syntheses of the masters of the thirteenth century remain, like the masterpieces of Gothic architecture, among the noblest constructions of the human mind. Nor was this immense effort wasted, if it is viewed as a stage in human evolution. It is difficult to grasp the extent to which the European mind was submerged in magic and superstition with the crumbling of Greco-Roman civilisation, until we compare the precision of thought of the great scholastics with their predecessors only two centuries earlier. The peoples of Europe had gone to school, and learned to think. As Whitehead pointed out in his lectures on 'Science and the Modern World', 'the Middle Ages formed one long training of the intellect of Western Europe in the sense of order'.

ROGER BACON

In the number and distinction of its thinkers in the scholastic period Oxford was second to none; and a special characteristic of English thought was its emphasis on mathematics and natural science. Only the reputation of Friar Bacon survived into the Renaissance as a forerunner of the scientific revolution; but it is now clear that Bacon himself was the product of a continuous line of thought which stretches back to Adelard of Bath, who in the first half of the twelfth century travelled in Spain, Sicily, Syria and Palestine and made contact with Arab science. In the second half of the twelfth century John of Salisbury, a luminary of the humanist school of Chartres, was complaining that Aristotle was causing a shift of interest from poetry and history to philosophy and science.

Bacon was a pupil of Grosseteste, and both Bacon and Grosseteste grasped the principles of scientific method. The deflation of theology as a science by William of Occam directed more

12 St Frideswide; window (14th century) in the Latin Chapel of
the Cathedral. Christ Church

attention to natural science. Between 1300 and 1360 a notable group of Merton masters, including Walter Burley and Thomas Bradwardine (later Archbishop of Canterbury), were questioning and revising Aristotelian concepts of physics and mechanics. Their work was known to the pioneers of modern science in the late sixteenth and early seventeenth century, including Galileo, and provides a direct link between medieval and modern science. Yet, with the possible exception of Roger Bacon, the scholastics were interested not in mastering nature but in demonstrating that nature was a symbol and part of the divine order.

Bacon, however, wrote that 'mathematics is the key and door of the science and things of this world'. 'Science of this kind is greater because it produces greater utilities.' He has long since lost to the Chinese his title to the invention of gunpowder, but in his *Epistola de Secretis Operibus* he predicts flying-machines, submarines, motor-cars. He wanted practical inventions as a means of repelling the Mongol invasion of Christendom – an interesting anticipation of the great rebound against the East which Europe was to make four centuries later.

13　Plato and Socrates; from a treatise on astronomy (St Albans, mid 13th century). Bodleian Library

14 Bastion in the city wall (*c.* 1100 and later). New College

2 The Earlier Colleges

In the second half of the thirteenth century we come to the first foundation of colleges. It is easy to overlook the fact that Paris, not Oxford, was the pioneer in the creation of colleges, with the foundation of the Hotel Dieu in 1180 and of the Sorbonne in 1257. But the colleges of the University of Paris never attained the status developed by the Oxford colleges by the end of the sixteenth century and they were swept away in the Revolution, whereas the colleges of Oxford and Cambridge survived, with their endowments, evolving and adapting themselves to every change, to make Oxford and Cambridge the leading examples of collegiate universities in the modern world.

There are now thirty-four colleges in Oxford, of varied character and history. Without embarking on the impossible task of doing justice to the history of every college, it is possible to explain the aims of the earlier founders and to pick out the foundations which influenced the general evolution of the colleges and of the University.

It becomes clear when we look at the first founders of colleges and their statutes that the need for the first colleges arose from the long and expensive training for the M.A. and the higher degrees of doctorates which has already been described. The academic predominance of the friars in the thirteenth century both alarmed and stimulated the older monastic orders and the secular clerks. With some three hundred friars in Oxford, of which one hundred might be university students, living in their own houses and supported by their orders, they were in a much more favourable position to reach higher degrees than the Benedictine monks or the secular clergy. With powerful backing from the Papacy, the friars pressed for the privileged position they had gained in Paris, that of taking degrees in theology without taking the degree in arts. This was resisted by the secular scholars, and the first written statute of the University in 1253 denied a degree in theology to any student who had not previously taken a degree in arts. But the friars frequently obtained dispensation from this provision, and there was constant complaint against powerful patrons of the friars, and 'letters from Lords sealed with wax'. The friars were also accused of deterring parents from sending their sons to Oxford, because the friars lured youths and even boys into their orders. The monastic orders reacted to this situation when in 1283 the southern province of the Benedictines founded Gloucester College (which, after the Reformation, became Worcester College) to house members of their monasteries studying in Oxford: the northern province followed in 1286 with the foundation of Durham College (later to become Trinity College). But they remained small in numbers and influence in the University.

It is of much greater importance and significance that nearly all the founders of the medieval secular colleges came from the class of the great ecclesiastical civil servants and statesmen. They were the men who over the centuries were building up the royal and national administration, until, under Henry VIII, it successfully challenged and swallowed the papal powers in England. A combination of motives led them to found colleges. As royal servants the founders accumulated substantial wealth (William of Wykeham at the height of his power had revenues worth about £100,000 a year in modern currency); celibacy debarred them from founding great families; they were aware of the importance of higher education in the University to provide successors of high calibre to carry on their life's work; to found a college which would perpetuate their name was a more attractive proposition than leaving their money to the University, which, in any case, with its rudimentary organisation, could hardly be trusted to manage it effectively.

William of Durham, who died in 1249, bequeathed in his will money to the University for the maintenance of ten or more Masters. He had been one of the Masters who migrated from Paris to Oxford in 1229 and was following the Paris example. According to the historian Matthew Paris, William 'abounded in great revenues but was gaping after greater' when he died. It was not till 1280 that the University established out of his bequest a definite community, and not till 1336 that it found a permanent home on the south side of High Street, as University College. Four Masters were to be chosen by the Chancellor and Masters to study theology (that is, the higher degree) and to live together. They were to be replaced as soon as they gained a benefice worth five marks a year, but the first four were to have a choice in the election of their successors.

In 1255 John of Balliol, a great lay magnate of the North, who was frequently at loggerheads with the Bishop of Durham, went so far as to kidnap the Bishop. For this he was made to do penance. In addition to being publicly scourged by the Bishop himself, he undertook to provide eightpence a day each for the maintenance of sixteen poor scholars at Oxford. It was not till 1282 that his widow, the Lady Dervorguilla, with the advice and guidance of her Franciscan confessor, gave her scholars a charter and endowment of land. Another century passed before they gained the status of a self-governing community. Till then the scholars were obliged to leave as soon as they gained their M.A., and they were chosen by two external Proctors or Rectors. In 1364 they successfully petitioned Pope Urban V for an alteration of the statutes; six of the scholars were allowed to proceed to the higher degree, and they were to elect a Master.

Walter de Merton, the first founder of a college endowed on a substantial scale, came from a burgess family in Basingstoke. It is uncertain whether he studied at Oxford, but he was presented to a living in 1233. He entered the royal chancery between 1236 and 1238. Between 1240 and 1247 he was in the service of Nicholas Farnham, Bishop of Durham. Returning to the royal chancery in 1247, Walter de Merton attained the position of King's Chancellor in 1261. As a king's man in the Barons' War, his career, his possessions, and his life were in danger. He therefore took the precaution in 1264 of assigning his manor in Malden, Surrey, for the support of students at Oxford. With the victory of the King his career rose to new heights. He was again Chancellor in 1272–4, and when Edward I was abroad at his accession, Walter de Merton was virtually acting as regent. He died in 1277 as Bishop of Rochester; his skeleton still surviving there shows that he was a man six feet in stature, truly a giant among medieval men in many ways.

In his later career, Walter de Merton had plenty of time and money to acquire property in Oxford, and to consider carefully the form of his foundation. He did not complete the final

16 Founder's cup (14th century). The Queen's College

hunundi factū: ut appetuc hūt
hununditatēs locoꝝ mag̃. alia
autē unuora que aquosa: dōu
venuat itũ deꝉius p̄iodi eius
teu. Cꝫ uī autē uctē tocū
tī quidīu quīdam p̄uuuacō
cōm uō tū g̃latōueu ꝓ coꝛp
cōm. li quidiu mauecat toiū
uctē ꝙadmod uaꝯ dicituꝉ. uō
eatē leuꝑ loca hununta ē uī
ꝛfluuunnus ꝛficta. Caiāiu
aꝉ. quod fit ꝗuos euuu lamuus
ātiꝗ̄ssimuos ec hōuu egꝩꝓs: loꝛ
regio tota fr̄a vietuꝛ ꝗ cr̄istꝰ
fluuu opus. aliꝰ f̄ regionem
ꝗ̄ãu alpiciēti: ꝗalaiu est ꝗ̃
ec rubrū maꝛe: arguuueutuuu
sufficiēus. hoc ē regū aliꝗui ꝓ
foꝺire atteuuptauit. Eꝗ̄o euu
gꝛas utiꝗ haleret ipis utilita
tes. uauugabit totus locus fr̄
dicituꝉ autē p̄uuus se-foꝝ couua
tiu fuisle. autiquoꝛ. fi uu veit
maꝛe ceis alcius terra: apt̃ ꝙ
ille p̄uuoꝛ cau̥ ꝓstiꝰ cellauut
fodieus: ut uō cōuꝑetuꝉ fluꝯ
fluuu cōuuꝓtio uuan. uuāuu
g̃ ꝙ̊ uuaꝛe ōia uuut huue cou
tuuuū ec ꝗ ꝙ̊d ꝛ que ē ho
biau uꝛauuau regio ueu h
uuuḣoꝛa vietuꝉ ꝗ ꝑfuuꝺioꝛe
ꝓter iōu uꝛfioꝛis regio uis
Ɋ.uuā aꝉ ꝙ̊d atteuuacōue fr̄a: fr̄a
ftagua ꝛ auta. teuuꝑe autē
ftō: ec ꝛelicta ꝛ ftaguata aqua
ꝺelicta ē ꝛ uuau aduuediata.
Cꝫ uō ꝛ que cū uueutideu ꝓ
ludeu addiceuut attꝛacōu fluꝯ
uuoꝛ tuuut: ut uuuto uuuuuoꝛe
uuaꝯ uuaguuutidiue. uꝉ uu
uuetat ado̥pauōu ꝗuꝉ āuo ler
agēuuuo. quare ec hoc facte uꝯ

cōuaꝉ acuupe. qꝝ p̄uuo lucit uu
ucra ftaguoꝝ: ꝛ hꝗ opus est fluuuoꝝ:
ꝛ caitē. ucte kꝫ ficuꝺ ouuue. Cꝰiof
autē uꝉftoꝛ leuuꝑ quidīu fluꝯ
uꝰ aꝛtian: ꝛ est adhuc kꝫ ocuꝉ uu
tcꝛe quo acuuꝰ uuotꝺ. Cꝫ uō
abafia uuteuꝛꝑꝺ uu faciefat. ꝗ
ꝓstiꝰ ftaguuu kr̄u fuut pꝛuuꝰ
p̄uuo: ꝺc uude ecfuacuuuu fuut uꝛꝯ.
Ɋoft lꝫ alia que abhoc uute̥ꝛ
cepto ꝛ ftaguuu abhac: ꝛ hoc leꝑ
fic acitī fifꝉ.lꝫ autēu kꝛʒ leꝑ uꝛ
celle teuuꝑe p̄leꝺetuꝉ.vei̥ꝺ fluuu
fieu uꝉftoꝛ.tauuꝺeu cꝝ alꝛt kꝫ ficut̃.
Caꝉalꝛ q̃ uuu ꝗu teuuꝑ uō te
fiat. ꝛ totu cr̄uuū: q̃ uꝉeꝗ ua
uuaus uꝉ uut꞊leuuꝑ fluꝛit. lete
ꝛat. aliꝗū fiet locus uu fluuꝛt.
oꝓ ē lꝫ ipoꝛ tertuuuut. teuuꝑul
autē uō lꝫt. fuɫꝛ ū hꝫ ꝛ uu aliuos
guut diec. Cꝛ veꝺ fiquidē
ꝛfluuu kr̄u ꝛ cōꝛūꝑuuetuꝛ. uu
leuuꝑ eadeu loca tcꝛe aquosa
u uaꝛe p̄uuutau. uctē liꝉ:uua
ꝛa hoc quidiu ꝺelerente.hoc
autēu fiꝗꝛedicēte leuuꝑ: uuā
kꝛu q̃ ouuꝯ tcꝛe uō leuuꝑ eadē
hc quiꝺ ꝗ̄ã fuit uuaꝛe lꝫ autē
auta.lꝫ p̄uuutautuꝉ teuuꝑe
ōꝛa. Cꝫ iua quidiu q̃ uou
leꝑ eadeu uucauta fuut tcꝛꝛe
uuatabuua fiꝛt ꝗ̄ꝓ qũ cauu lꝫ
acidiut dicituꝉ est.liꝉ autēu ꝗꝓ
ꝙ̊ buu quiꝺ ꝓeuuu.bu ā uō kꝫ
fluuoꝛ.

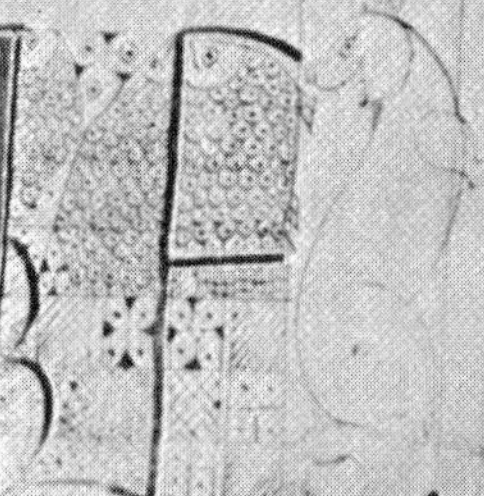

form of the statutes till 1274. Preference was to be given to founders' kin, and after them to candidates from the diocese of Winchester: and in fact the first Fellows of Merton to reside in Oxford were the eight nephews of Walter de Merton. The number of Fellows soon rose to twenty-five. The fact that the founder forbade his scholars to take vows or enter a cloister and that he enjoined those who prospered in the world not to be unmindful of the interests of the House, shows that Walter de Merton designed his foundation primarily to strengthen the secular priesthood, and to encourage men who would follow in his own footsteps as great servants of Church and State.

The main aim of the foundation was to enable the scholars (or Fellows) to proceed to the degree of M.A. and the higher degree of theology. But as early as 1270, twelve 'poor secondary scholars' were to be supported on a benefaction promised by Richard of Cornwall, Henry III's brother. On his death in 1271, the benefaction did not materialise, and the number of poor secondary scholars dwindled. In 1380 they were revived by a benefaction of a Sub-Warden of Merton as twelve portionists (or postmasters) maintained at a rate lower than that of the Fellows. These Merton 'poor secondary scholars' and 'portionists' appear to be the first example on a small scale of undergraduate students attached to a college.

The peculiar importance of Walter de Merton as a founder was not merely the scale and liberality of his foundation, or the magnificence of his chapel and buildings, which arose in Merton Street, but the fact that he established with such firmness, deliberation and detail the constitution of a self-governing community that it became the pattern for subsequent foundations. This self-government was to be balanced by a powerful Visitor, no less than the Archbishop of Canterbury. He was to select the Warden from a list of three nominated by the seven senior Fellows, and could in extreme cases remove him. Three Fellows were to act as Bursars, and there was to be a careful audit of accounts.

It is unnecessary to enter into the tedious question of the exact precedence of foundation of the three colleges of University, Balliol and Merton. A more interesting point arises from the closeness of the dates of foundation. It is a curious coincidence that William of Durham and Nicholas Farnham, who was one of Walter de Merton's patrons, were both Masters who migrated from Paris in 1229, and that Kirkham, who was in effect the initiator of the Balliol foundation, was Nicholas Farnham's successor as Bishop of Durham. Through the mists of time, one gets the impression that these early founders were all part of a select élite of statesmen, aware of each other, sharing the same interests and ideals.

EXETER, ORIEL, QUEEN'S

Walter of Stapeldon, Bishop of Exeter, founder of Stapeldonhalle, later to be known as Exeter College, was not as lucky as Walter de Merton. Walter of Stapeldon was a prominent minister of Edward II, and at the fall of that ill-fated monarch he was seized and beheaded by the mob in Cheapside. In addition to bequeathing funds for grammar schools in Exeter and Ashburton, he had in the days of his greatness given small revenues in Cornwall for establishing a Hall in Oxford for students from the West country. Eight Fellows from Devonshire and four from Cornwall were to qualify in arts and philosophy for work in Church or State. They were to vacate their fellowships as soon as they had gained their M.A. and lectured as Necessary Regents or obtained a benefice. Till 1384 their Rector was elected annually. The Fellows lived at first in Hart Hall in Catte Street, purchased by the bishop, and then moved to the present site of the college in the Turl. The chapel was consecrated in the bishop's lifetime.

17   Page of a manuscript of Aristotle (Oxford, *c.* 1350). Balliol College

Another of Edward II's leading officials, Adam de Brome, Rector of the University Church of St Mary's and a clerk of the royal chancery, founded Oriel College in 1324. In 1326 it was confirmed by royal charter, and the King assigned to it the advowson of St Mary's and made Adam de Brome the first Provost of the College. The statutes followed the model of Merton: the scholars and Fellows of bachelor standing were to proceed to M.A., and then to the higher degrees of theology or law. A few months later the powerful Bishop of Lincoln, a leader of the Queen's faction, intervened and secured a revision of the statutes which displaced the Crown in favour of the Bishop of Lincoln as Visitor. In the eighteenth century, however, a legal judgment confirmed the royal statutes of 1326, and Oriel remains a royal foundation, with the Crown as its Visitor.

Robert de Eglesfield, founder of Queen's College, was a lesser landowner in Cumberland; by 1331 he was a royal clerk and later chaplain to Queen Philippa, wife of Edward III. In 1341, six months after the start of Edward III's war with the French, Eglesfield obtained a charter for a 'hall of the Queen's scholars at Oxford' in the parish of St Peter's in the East. Queen Philippa was described as patroness and co-foundress. Eglesfield's statutes have a strong flavour of the overblown chivalry of Edward III's court. Just as Edward III's Knights of the Garter were to sit at a round table to imitate King Arthur, Eglesfield's scholars were to sit on three sides of an oblong table to symbolise the Last Supper. They were to wear blood-red robes to symbolise the Crucifixion; they were to be twelve in number, representing the Apostles, and the poor-boys and choristers were to be seventy-two, symbolising the disciples. Eglesfield was insistent on courtliness of manner and mode of life, and envisaged emoluments and a standard of living of the scholars much higher than those of his predecessors. 'Believing that men well instructed in theology strengthen the Catholic faith, adorn the Church universal, and keep the Christian people in peace', Eglesfield ordained that his scholars were to study theology, one being permitted to take canon law, and if they did not take their Doctor's degree within eighteen years, they were to leave. Preference in election was to be given to natives of Cumberland and Westmorland.

The magnificence of Eglesfield's scheme bore no relation to his resources; he was not a rich pluralist on the scale of Walter de Merton, or later, William of Wykeham. But he could remind the Queen of her obligations, and he had generous friends who responded to his enthusiasm. A royal charter gave the Wardenship of St Julian's Hospital in Southampton to the college; centuries later it was to make the college wealthy when the site and lands were swallowed by the Southampton docks. Eglesfield himself acted as the first Provost, struggling to put the college on its feet. There were so few Fellows that the college was nearly wiped out in the Black Death, and the number did not rise above seven or eight till the end of the fifteenth century; the poor-boys remained a handful. The college made ends meet by letting rooms to commensales, paying guests who were usually Masters and Doctors.

Eglesfield's more exotic fantasies were soon dispelled by the brisk north-country air brought by his scholars, and the medieval college buildings were completely replaced in the eighteenth century.

But the college rightly venerates its courageous and pious founder and his Queen, agreed by all contemporaries to be 'that full noble and good woman'. His drinking-horn is still the college loving-cup, and the college is still summoned to dine by trumpet.

18 The Virgin and Child; glass in the east window of Merton College Chapel (15th century)

19 *(opposite)* Head of a bishop (14th
    century) from the Church of St Mary
    the Virgin. New College Cloister
20 William of Wykeham's crozier
    (14th century). New College

William of Wykeham, founder of New College, ranks in importance and originality with Walter de Merton. Of peasant origin, William went through grammar school at Winchester but did not proceed to the University. By 1351 he had become Surveyor of the King's Works, responsible for the large alterations at Windsor. He rose to be the most powerful royal civil servant of his time, which was a period of political instability and social unrest aggravated by the war with France and the ravages of plague. In 1367 he became Bishop of Winchester, but even before that Froissart wrote of him: 'At this time there reigned a Priest called William of Wykeham. This William of Wykeham was so much in favour with the King that everything was done by him and nothing was done without him.' From 1367 to 1370 he was Lord Chancellor, but in 1376 he was attacked by John of Gaunt's faction and accused of mismanagement and embezzlement. With the accession of Richard II he was restored to favour and an active post in government, and was again Chancellor from 1389 to 1391. Until his death in 1404, he kept clear of politics and the events leading to the deposition of Richard II.

From the time he became Bishop of Winchester, he was laying down his plans for the twin foundations of a grammar school at Winchester and a college at Oxford. In 1369 he began to purchase land in Oxford, and in 1379 he started a small school at Winchester. The charter of foundation at Oxford was issued in 1379, and the buildings were substantially completed by 1386.

As a former Surveyor of the King's Works, William of Wykeham took a keen interest in architectural planning. His buildings therefore laid down for the first time the pattern of a quadrangle containing all the requirements of a collegiate life. The hall and chapel were placed end to end on the north side, with an ante-chapel replacing a nave, the entrance-tower and the muniment tower balancing each other to the west and east, and the scholars' chambers on the south side. It was an example of planning which powerfully influenced subsequent foundations. In view of the troubled times, it also seems to have taken account of the needs of defence.

In his statutes William of Wykeham explains his aims. He wished to help in curing 'the general disease of the clerical army, which we have observed to be grievously wounded owing to the fewness of the clergy, arising from pestilences, wars and other miseries of the world'. He had noted the decline in numbers at Oxford, which used to produce 'men of great learning, fruitful to the Church of God and to the king and Realm'. He observed that grammar is 'reputed to be the first of the arts or liberal sciences and is the foundation, door, and opening of all other liberal arts and sciences'. He therefore took the logical step, already tentatively foreshadowed in the foundations of Walter de Merton and of Robert de Eglesfield, of providing a grammar school at Winchester to prepare students for Oxford, and a college at Oxford which would provide not only for the attainment of higher degrees but for the maintenance and teaching of undergraduates through their arts course. Only a minority of his seventy scholars and Fellows at New College would remain for the higher degrees for which they were required to take priests' orders within the year of their M.A.: the majority would go into the outside world and work in church and state. The Warden and the senior Fellows would select the candidates from Winchester; after two years on probation they became Fellows, with a vote at college meetings. In this democratic society ranging from eighteen years upwards, discipline, guidance and the supervision of study were largely in the hands of the Sub-Warden, the three Bursars, and the five Deans who arranged for the seniors to act as

21 Lion and pelican; figures (*c.* 1509) crowning buttresses on the
west cloister in the Great Quadrangle. Magdalen College

magistri informatores to the junior Fellows. In the medieval period, there were on average about thirty to fifty-five undergraduate members, and twenty Bachelors.

By providing in his two linked colleges at Oxford and Winchester for the whole range of secondary and higher education, and by mixing seniors and juniors in New College, William of Wykeham created the prototype of the post-Reformation college, which was undergraduate as well as graduate. The tutorial system by which the seniors took responsibility for the teaching as well as the discipline of the juniors was the logical consequence of the composition of the college. So confident was William of Wykeham of the superiority of his system of teaching that he forbade his Fellows to supplicate for any graces or dispensation in regard to degrees from the University. In 1607 this provision was interpreted curiously and perversely to exempt New College men from taking university examinations. This privilege, which was also asserted by King's College at Cambridge, was not surrendered till 1834, by which time it had seriously undermined the academic standing of the college.

Lincoln College, founded in 1429 by Richard Fleming, Bishop of Lincoln, was in origin a reversion to the earlier type of purely graduate college. The seven Fellows, in addition to the Rector, were to be Masters studying theology, except for one Canonist, and Bachelors were only to be elected if there was not a supply of Masters. Fleming had been Proctor of Oxford University, active in opposition to Archbishop Arundel's visitation in 1411 to stamp out Wyclifism, and had himself been suspected of Wyclifite opinions. He soon won preferment by showing himself to be the champion of the Church and the Papacy. He declared the object of his foundation to be the defence of orthodoxy against the 'swinish snouts who presumed to feed upon its precious pearls'.

The name of All Souls College, prescribed by its founder, Henry Chichele, recalls the closing epoch of the Middle Ages, splendid but doomed to decay. By the terms of the royal charter of 1438, the Fellows were to 'pray for the soul of Henry v, and all those who fell in the war for the Crown of France'. Chichele was educated at Winchester, and was one of the early Fellows of New College in 1386, and took his doctorate in law. He won the favour of both Pope and King Henry v, who promoted him to the see of Canterbury in 1419, which he was to hold for nearly thirty years. He was godfather to the infant King Henry vi. A diplomatist and statesman, Chichele was less original and more conservative in his views on education than William of Wykeham. His forty Fellows were to be elected from candidates who had already studied for three years in the faculty of arts or law, and they were to proceed to the higher degrees of theology or law: as an eminent legist, Chichele stipulated that a proportion of his Fellows were to study canon and civil law. Founder's kin and candidates from counties where the college held property were to have preference. He hoped that his college would produce eminent servants of church and state as well as learned men, and over the centuries his hopes have not been disappointed. He recalled in his statutes the time when 'both the Services [i.e., church and state] competing in pious emulation, made the kingdom of England formidable to its adversaries, and resplendent and glorious among nations abroad'. There is more than a hint here of the nationalism emerging from the Hundred Years' War; and from another angle, Chichele's foundation foreshadows Wolsey and the Tudors. The college was amply endowed from the start with the lands of suppressed alien priories bought by Chichele from the Crown. All Souls is the only college of medieval foundation which has retained its original character as a graduate college.

Two factors may have contributed to this survival; a restricted site in the heart of Oxford discouraged expansion; the college's rich endowments gave no incentive to take responsibility

22 Statue of the Virgin (*c.* 1424). Merton College Chapel
23 *(overleaf)* East range of the Front Quadrangle (1438–44). All Souls College

for undergraduates and fee-paying pupils: the special connection of the foundation with the Crown and the law made its Fellows look towards a public, rather than a cloistered, career.

MAGDALEN, BRASENOSE, CORPUS CHRISTI

In his foundation of Magdalen College, William Waynflete carried further the conceptions of William of Wykeham. Waynflete was Master of Winchester 1429–42 and Provost of Eton from 1443. Highly in favour with King Henry VI, he became Bishop of Winchester in 1447 and Chancellor in 1456. He obtained a licence to found a Hall in Oxford in 1448, but it was not till near his death in 1486 that he delivered to the college the final form of its statutes. There is no indication that he had been educated at Winchester or New College, but in the course of his career he had become familiar with his predecessor's work, and his statutes often copy the wording of those of New College. But there were important differences and developments. In contrast to Winchester, Waynflete placed his grammar school in Oxford, adjacent to the college: it was to be open to suitable candidates without restriction. There were to be seventy scholars on the foundation, as at New College, but of these, thirty were to be Demies, so-called because their rate of maintenance was half that of the seniors. They could be admitted at an age not earlier than twelve, and could stay not later than the age of twenty-five. It was not intended that they should have a claim to proceed to full fellowships, and in the early days of the college few did so; it was only at the end of the sixteenth century that the practice grew up of admitting them to fellowships in regular succession.

There was also express provision for not more than twenty commensales, fee-paying students not on the foundation, who were to be the sons of nobles or worthy persons. Whereas William of Wykeham's scholars, entering New College at the age of fifteen, and more likely at seventeen or eighteen as probationer-fellows, were more like the modern graduate student or Junior Research Fellow, Waynflete's Demies and commensales are recognisably what we mean today by undergraduate scholars and commoners.

The third distinctive feature of the Magdalen statutes is the greater scale of provision of teaching within the college. The Demies were to be well-grounded in grammar and receive tuition from the more senior Demies. There were to be three Praelectors to teach the Fellows the more advanced subjects of theology and natural and moral philosophy, with substantial fixed stipends: they need not necessarily be Fellows of the college, and they were to be selected by open competition. Their lectures were also to be open to the whole university. All these new features in the constitution of Magdalen point the way to the decisive shift which was to take place between the Reformation and the Civil War by which the colleges took over from the Halls and from the University the major share in the responsibility for housing and teaching undergraduates. In 1360 the existing colleges contained only forty M.A.s, twenty-three B.A.s and ten undergraduates; by 1552 there were only eight Halls left.

Following the example of Magdalen, the statutes of Brasenose College and Corpus Christi College provided for undergraduate members of the college and their tuition. Brasenose was founded jointly by William Smyth and Richard Sutton, incorporating the existing Brasenose Hall, and received its charter in 1512. Smyth was in the service of the Lady Margaret, mother of Henry VII, and after the victory of Bosworth was appointed to office under the Crown, became a member of the King's Council, Bishop of Lichfield, and finally of Lincoln. Richard Sutton was a distinguished lawyer, and Steward of the important and aristocratic Nunnery of Syon, near London. He outlived Smyth and revised the bishop's original statutes in 1522.

There was no provision for undergraduate scholars comparable to the Magdalen Demies, but six sons of noblemen were to be admitted at their own cost or that of the college, and put under the charge of a tutor. In 1552 the list of members of colleges attributes seventy members to Brasenose, of which a considerable proportion must have been undergraduate.

The founder of Corpus Christi College, Richard Fox, owed his career, like Bishop Smyth, to Henry VII. He studied in Paris, where he met the exiled Henry, Earl of Richmond. He was present at the battle of Bosworth and rose rapidly to be Lord Privy Seal and Bishop, successively, of Exeter, Durham and Winchester. A deed of 1513 records that he was planning a monastic college at Oxford for eight monks from St Swithin's, Winchester. It was the advice of his friend Hugh Oldham, Bishop of Exeter, that altered his plan. Oldham was a Lancashire man, notable for his foundation of Manchester Grammar School; he also contributed a large sum, £ 4,100, to the foundation of Bishop Fox's college. It is recorded by Holinshed, the Elizabethan chronicler, that Oldham pointed out, 'Shall we build houses and provide livelihoods for a company of bussing monks, whose end and fall we ourselves may see?' Bishop Fox delivered his charter and statutes of the college in 1517. Besides twenty Fellows, there were to be twenty discipuli, chosen at the age of 12–17. A discipulus shared a room with a Fellow, who acted as his tutor; as a candidate for a fellowship he had a certain preference to external candidates. Six sons of noblemen could also be admitted as fee-paying students. Like Magdalen, there was provision for the endowment of three Readers in Latin, Greek, and Theology, whose lectures were to be open to the whole university. The Corpus statutes are notable for the first endowment of the teaching of Greek and the emphasis on the study of the New Testament, thereby recording the advance of the new learning in Oxford. But Fox says in his statutes that the intention of his foundation was 'solely or mainly for the sake of theology', and the statutes required Fellows to take orders when they proceeded to the M.A. degree.

THE FIRST UNIVERSITY BUILDINGS

In the fifteenth century the University was also equipping itself with buildings, though it had much more difficulty in attracting benefactions than the colleges. The earliest university building was the fourteenth-century Congregation House on the north side of the chancel of the University Church of St Mary, which also housed the University Library. In 1439 the Abbot of Oseney built a substantial range of new schools and lecture-rooms, rented by the Masters, in Schools Street, the site of the present Bodleian Quadrangle and Divinity School. In 1427 the University purchased the site for the Divinity School from Balliol College and slowly collected the funds for building by public appeal and subscription. The Divinity School was not completed till about 1480, and in the meantime the plan was enlarged to provide for the rich donation of several hundred books from the library of Duke Humphrey of Gloucester, youngest brother of Henry V. His library was the finest collection in the country, and reflected the Duke's interest in the new learning spreading from Italy.

The Duke's interest in Oxford was stimulated by Gilbert Kymer, his physician, who had been Principal of Hart Hall and Chancellor of the University. The Duke had promised to provide £ 100 for the building of a new library over the Divinity School, but his benefaction was not completed when he died suddenly in 1447. The University boldly pressed on with their plan, and other patrons, such as Bishop Kemp of London, came to the rescue. The new library, commemorating the name of Duke Humphrey, was probably completed by 1488.

25 Duke Humphrey's Library (late 15th century). Bodleian Library

26 South doorway of
St Mary's Chapel
(*c.* 1521). Hertford
College

27 *(opposite)* Bernard Van
Orley, *Christ Bearing the
Cross;* detail of an
altarpiece (*c.* 1530).
Oriel College

The splendour of these late medieval buildings of the University and the colleges masks the fact that in the fifteenth century the University declined both in numbers and reputation. Not only was there a general decline of population after the plagues of the fourteenth century, but Cambridge was now a vigorous competitor. Oxford also suffered from its association with the heresy of Wyclif. But Wyclif himself and the Lollard movement must be regarded as a symptom of more general causes affecting not only England but Europe as a whole.

John Wyclif, as a Bachelor and not yet a Master, was a junior Fellow of Merton in 1356 and in 1360 became Master of Balliol. A year later he resigned this position on receiving the college living of Fillingham. By 1363 he was back in Oxford with a licence of absence from his parish, and occupied rooms in Queen's College as a commensalis. In 1365 he was appointed Master of Canterbury College, recently founded as a mixed community of monks and secular clergy. It was an unhappy experiment, as the two sides did not mix, and the monks secured Wyclif's dismissal as Master. By 1372 Wyclif had established a reputation as the leading Master in the Schools. In the middle of the fourteenth century there was a strong conservative reaction led by the great Masters Bradwardine and Fitz Ralph, Archbishop of Armagh, in Oxford against the 'new way', the logic of William of Occam, which divorced theology from philosophy. Wyclif pushed this reaction further, and by his vigorous assertion that 'the existence of God can be proved by infallible proof by a pure philosopher' rekindled the enthusiasm of the students. Ultimately Wyclif's philosophical ideas led him to doubt the eucharistic doctrine of transubstantiation.

If the controversy caused by Wyclif's ideas had remained on the academic plane, it would have created no great stir, but it was a different matter when he entered the political scene under the patronage of John of Gaunt, leader of the anti-clerical party which pressed for an increase of clerical taxation and even confiscation of church and monastic property. By 1378 Wyclif had preached in the London churches against the 'possessioners', the wealthy clergy and monastic houses, and expounded in tracts his doctrine of Dominion – that clerical property was justified only by grace and that if it was abused, it could be taken away. Bishop Courtenay's move to indict him before Convocation at St Paul's in 1378 remained inconclusive owing to John of Gaunt's protection. Meanwhile Wyclif had been denounced to the Pope, who issued bulls of condemnation to the King, to the Archbishop, and to the University. At the beginning of 1381, the Chancellor of the University appointed a commission which condemned Wyclif's doctrines by a bare majority. He refused to recant and until his death in 1384 he continued to pour out tracts of an increasingly extreme and provocative character. By then he had enunciated in advance some of the main themes of the Protestant Reformers of the sixteenth century – repudiation of papal authority, dissolution of the monasteries, denial of the Real Presence in the Eucharist, reliance on the literal word of scripture translated for the common people.

The timing of Wyclif's final plunge into heresy, and the consequences, were unfortunate. A few months after his formal condemnation by the University, in June 1381, the Peasants' Revolt broke out. For a moment the whole social fabric seemed to be dissolving, when London was only saved from wholesale destruction by the calm courage of the boy King Richard, and Archbishop Sudbury was lynched by Wat Tyler's peasant horde. The propertied classes, lay and clerical, closed their ranks and found in Wyclif and his Oxford supporters a scapegoat. The University had to face the first determined attack on its independence. For the first time in England, the methods of the Inquisition were imported with the passing of the statute on the burning of heretics in 1401.

In the long run Wyclif and the Lollard movement ruled out a gradual reform of the Church and ensured that the dissolution of the monasteries should come about in a much more clumsy and wasteful form.

In 1382 the Chancellor of the University, Rygge, was summoned by Courtenay, the successor of the murdered Sudbury as Archbishop of Canterbury, and the royal council, to publish the decrees banning Wyclif and his followers from teaching. In the following year Courtenay held a Convocation of his province at Oxford, and the Chancellor became a member of a committee to enquire into the teaching of senior members of the University. By a combination of firmness and tact Courtenay had succeeded in breaking or at least driving underground Wyclif's support in the University. Oxford remained suspect to the government as the Lollard movement spread in the country, and became associated with open treason in the conspiracy of Sir John Oldcastle in 1414. In 1408 Archbishop Arundel put pressure on the Chancellor to burn Wyclif's books and to order a monthly inquisition to discover heretics in all colleges and Halls. In 1411 the Archbishop's assertion of his right to make a visitation of the University provoked open defiance: the Proctors fortified the Church of St Mary's against the Archbishop's entry. The King required the resignation of the Chancellor and Proctors, and the papal bull exempting the University from ecclesiastical jurisdiction was revoked by King, Parliament and Pope in turn.

This atmosphere of suspicion and unorthodoxy was not conducive to a free and vigorous intellectual life and may have deterred students from entering Oxford. The Hundred Years' War cut Oxford off from Paris, and for the first time forced on it a provincial outlook. With the Great Schism of the papacy beginning in 1378 and the increasing outcry against papal provision to benefices, Oxford Masters found it increasingly difficult to obtain benefices. The bastard feudalism of the fifteenth century brought aristocratic pressure on the University in appointments and dispensations for degrees.

A deeper cause of malaise, common to the whole of Europe, was the creeping paralysis and death which was overtaking the medieval scholastic philosophy. An Oxford scholar in the early fifteenth century lamented that 'that subtle and lovely philosophy which formerly made our mother the University glorious throughout the world, has almost totally been lulled to sleep'. Fortunately it was not long before a new breath of intellectual life came from the Italy of the Renaissance.

29 Eight signs of the zodiac; carved bosses from the Fitzjames Gatehouse (*c.* 1500). Merton College

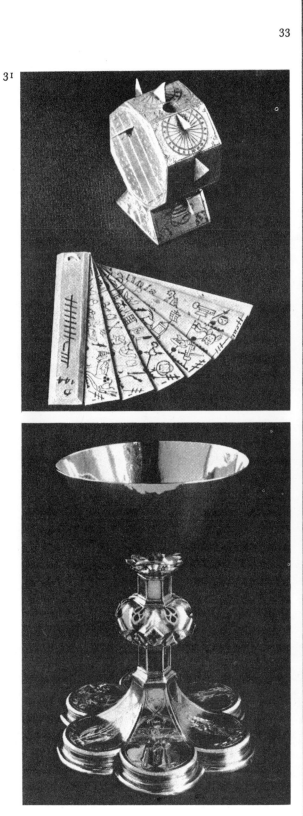

30   *(opposite)* Detail from a Flemish tapestry (*c.* 1500) showing the betrothal of Prince Arthur and Catharine of Aragon. Magdalen College

31   Cardinal Wolsey's dial and Archbishop Laud's clog almanack. Museum of the History of Science

32   Bishop Fox's chalice (1507). Corpus Christi College

33   Bishop Fox's crozier (*c.* 1490). Corpus Christi College

34 Quadrangle of St Edmund Hall (16th and 17th centuries)

3 Renaissance and Reformation

In the fifteenth century Italy regained the intellectual leadership in Europe, which she had lost in the thirteenth. A secular, urban society was prepared to absorb the values of the Greco-Roman world. The continuity with the ancient world had never been wholly lost, as is obvious when we look at the evolution of Italian architecture; in Italy the Romanesque and Renaissance styles emerge naturally from the Roman, while the Gothic style is in Italy an awkward intruder. In the thirteenth century the Emperor Frederick II, 'stupor mundi', wrote the first scientific treatise on the art of hawking, and designed a purely classical gateway for his great castle of Castel Monte in Apulia. In the first half of the fifteenth century Italian humanists were eagerly searching out Greek manuscripts, and encouraging a flow of scholars and texts from a doomed Constantinople.

The full impact of the humanist new learning did not reach England till the period 1490–1520, but throughout the fifteenth century the way was being prepared by a handful of notable patrons and scholars. Duke Humphrey of Gloucester, the younger brother of Henry V, attracted Italian humanists to his service, and was in constant touch with Italy about the purchase of books. Though King's College, Cambridge, got the Latin books which Gloucester had bequeathed to Oxford in his will, his gifts to Oxford in his lifetime gave the biggest single impetus to the new learning in Oxford. Two other notable lay patrons had Oxford connections. John Tiptoft who became the Yorkist Earl of Worcester in 1449 was a commensalis at University College in 1440. He had studied in Padua, and his collection of books was second only to Gloucester's. Beheaded in the Lancastrian *revanche* of 1470, he left books in his will both to Oxford and Cambridge. George Neville, the younger brother of Warwick the Kingmaker, was a student at Balliol, Chancellor of the University in 1453, Archbishop of York in 1465; he brought to England the refugee scholar Emanuel the Greek, and may himself have learnt Greek.

Of scholars, Robert Flemmyng, nephew of the founder of Lincoln College, studied at Padua, learnt Greek and left books to Lincoln College. William Grey, a student at Balliol, Chancellor of the University in 1447, and later Bishop of Ely, studied at Padua and Ferrara, and left an important collection of books, including classical texts, to Balliol College. He encouraged John Free, Fellow of Balliol, to go to Padua: of whom it can be said that he is the first English humanist in the fifteenth century to compete on equal terms with the Italians. Thomas Chaundler, Warden of New College 1454–75, was a noted latinist, and used his influence to promote an interest in the new learning.

Following this handful of pioneers, the leaders in the reception of the new learning were

William Grocin, Thomas Linacre, John Colet, Thomas More, and Erasmus. Grocin, educated at Winchester and New College, and Reader in divinity at Magdalen College, went to Italy in 1481, and lectured on Greek at Oxford in 1491–3. Linacre of All Souls joined Grocin in Italy, became physician to Henry VIII, founded the College of Physicians in 1518, and endowed in his will lectureships in medicine at both Oxford and Cambridge. Colet, after studying abroad, lectured at Oxford on the Epistles, became Dean of St Paul's in 1505, and in 1509 founded St Paul's School, appointing William Lily, an accomplished scholar in both Greek and Latin, as High Master in 1512. More left Oxford to study at the Inns of Court, and was thus destined for a lay and legal career, which led him both to the Chancellorship and martyrdom under Henry VIII. The famous Dutchman Erasmus spent much time both at Oxford and Cambridge, and was the friend of More, Colet and Linacre. He wrote enthusiastically about the progress of the new learning in England:

> When I hear my Colet, I seem to be listening to Plato himself. In Grocin who does not marvel at such a perfection of learning. What can be more acute, profound and delicate than the judgment of Linacre? What has Nature ever created more gentle, more sweet, more happy than the genius of Thomas More?

WOLSEY, HENRY VIII, AND THE REFORMATION

This was the brief spring-time of the Renaissance before the gathering tempest of the Reformation darkened the sky. In England the connection between the Renaissance and Reformation was particularly close. The urge to acquire the new learning was in many cases theological; the key to a true, primitive Christianity was to be the study of the New Testament in Greek. Colet, Erasmus and More poured scorn on the schoolmen and the monks, and thereby helped to create that climate of opinion which enabled Henry VIII and Thomas Cromwell, with an ease which surprised even them, to topple over the worm-eaten structure of monasticism and papal bureaucracy. But even Henry VIII could not control the doctrinal passions of the Reformation. If in the sixteenth century the English people escaped a full-scale religious war, they had to experience the dismal ordeal of denunciations, iconoclasm, executions and burnings which marred the reigns of Henry VIII, Edward VI and Mary. In 1555 Latimer, Ridley and Cranmer were burned at the stake in Oxford in front of the gates of Balliol College.

It would not have been surprising if Oxford, never far from the centre of the storms of the Reformation, had foundered altogether. In the course of the century the University had to undergo no less than five government visitations: but not all were hostile or unconstructive. The number of students fell in the period 1530–60. Severely buffeted, the University survived, and under Elizabeth it expanded.

As early as 1521 younger Fellows at both universities were being infected with Lutheran ideas. William Tyndale who took his M.A. at Magdalen Hall in 1515, was 'privily expounding' the New Testament to Fellows of Magdalen. He moved to Cambridge, then to Germany, to meet Luther and complete his translation into English of the New Testament. In 1526 smuggled copies were denounced and burnt by a conference of bishops in London. In 1536 he was betrayed to the imperial authorities in Antwerp, and burnt by the Inquisition. His posthumous influence on the language and religion of the English-speaking peoples has been incalculable: for his translation of the New Testament was included in the 'Matthew Bible' which was later licensed by Henry VIII for sale in England, and it formed the basis and model for the Authorised Version of 1611.

The conservative schoolmen in Oxford attacked the young enthusiasts of the new learning, and proclaimed a war of the 'Trojans against the Greeks'. Tyndale wrote to Thomas More that 'the old barking curs, Duns' disciples and like draff called Scotists, the children of darkness, raged in every pulpit against Greek, Latin and Hebrew'. Thomas More, backed by Wolsey and the King, came down on the side of the new learning. But in 1528 Thomas Garret, later to be burned at Smithfield in the Marian reaction, and John Clark in Wolsey's own new foundation of Cardinal College were arrested for disseminating heretical literature and opinions. In 1530 the two universities were ordered by the King to appoint committees to search for suspected books, including English translations of the Bible.

CHRIST CHURCH

In 1529 the fall of Wolsey, the last, the most powerful and the most magnificent of the ecclesiastical statesmen and founders of colleges in the tradition of Walter de Merton and Wykeham, threatened his grand foundation of Cardinal College with extinction. Wolsey had started his career as Fellow and Bursar of Magdalen College, and Master of Magdalen College School. His statutes reflect the influence of Waynflete and Fox; four censors were to supervise studies in the subjects of philosophy, dialectic, literae humaniores, theology, law and medicine.

In 1524 the Pope had empowered Wolsey to dissolve St Frideswide and twenty other houses to provide for the new college: the charter was issued and the foundation stone laid in 1525. In 1530, shortly before his death, Wolsey writes to the King 'humbly and on my knees with weeping eyes to recommend unto your excellent charity and goodness the poor College of Oxford'. In 1532 the college was reprieved, and refounded as 'King's College', but it was to be an ecclesiatical, rather than an educational, foundation. In 1541 the King remarked that 'our universitie of Oxenfort hath of late days by lack of ordre fallen into no small ruin and decaye as well in learning as in vertues, behavor, and good manners'. In 1546, shortly before his death, the King finally made up his mind about the foundation. The new cathedral see of Oxford, at first destined to be sited at the dissolved Abbey of Oseney, was combined with the college, reconstituted as 'Ecclesia Christi Cathedralis Oxon', and the new foundation was endowed with a revenue of £2,000 per annum, mostly from the former lands of Oseney. Wolsey's educational aims were revived: there were to be one hundred Students [i.e. Fellows] and five Regius Professorships of Divinity, Hebrew, Greek, Civil Law and Medicine.

DISSOLUTION OF THE MONASTERIES

The fall of Wolsey and the royal divorce had precipitated the Reformation. With some resistance from the Faculty of Arts, quelled by governmental pressure, the University had given its opinion that the marriage of Henry and Catharine of Aragon was illegal. In 1534 the University declared that the Pope, being merely 'Episcopus Romanus', had no jurisdiction in England. In January 1535 the King assumed the title of Supreme Head of the Church, and Thomas Cromwell as Vicar-General wielded the power. The comparative ease with which the dissolution of the monasteries was carried out was largely due to Cromwell's brilliant timing and cynical opportunism in exploiting anti-clerical opinion, judiciously combining the carrot and the stick. The valuation and visitation of the monasteries in 1535 were followed by the suppression of the lesser houses: the time of the greater houses came in 1538. Abbots and priors were appeased or bribed with large pensions or preferments into surrendering their houses; the few who resisted were ruthlessly killed. There was no resistance in Oxford: the Abbots of Oseney and Abingdon, the Abbess of Godstow, the monastic colleges and the friars peaceably surrendered their houses. Dr London, Warden of New College, was an active and hated Visitor in 1538, described by his opponents as 'a stout and filthy Prebendary'.

The universities were involved in the general Visitation of 1535 and Cromwell was able to exploit the division of opinion in the universities, and also between them. Under the influence of Erasmus and Luther, Cambridge was by now more committed to the new learning and the Reformation than Oxford. Cambridge was to supply most of the Protestant martyrs in the Marian persecution, including Ridley, Latimer and Cranmer. The two Visitors of the universities were Cambridge men, Layton and Leigh, with strong sympathy for the new learning and contempt for scholasticism. Layton wrote to Cromwell, 'In New College we have established a lecturer in Greek and another in Latin with an honest salary and stipend…Wee have set Dunce [i.e. Duns Scotus] in Bocardo and have utterly banished him from Oxford forever, with all his blynd glosses, and is now made a common servant to every man, fast nayled up upon posts in all common houses of easement.' The Visitors ordered public lecturers to be established in Greek, Latin and Civil Law at the Colleges of All Souls, Magdalen, Merton and Queen's. The colleges were relieved of the payment of first-fruits and tenths on condition that they contributed to the support of a King Henry VIII's Lecturer. The University had therefore not too much cause to complain of the visitation of Layton and Leigh: the more odious side of their activities was reserved for the monasteries. But the suppression of the monasteries, their houses and colleges in Oxford was bound to arouse fears of an attack on college endowments. The King, however, was already prepared to reassure the universities on this point; as an exponent of Renaissance monarchy he was not lacking in a sense of the value of education. Both the King and Cromwell were prepared to use the shrewd strategy of appeasing interests which were not too weak to be bullied.

In 1549, however, a major Visitation was planned. The Visitation of the universities ordered by King Edward VI was headed by Dudley, Earl of Warwick, but the most important Visitor at Oxford was Cox, the Dean of Christ Church. Armed with an elaborate draft code of instructions, the Visitors spent several months in discussion with the University and colleges. In the outcome, the more drastic proposals in the instructions for amalgamating colleges, or allocating particular colleges to the study of particular subjects such as law or medicine, fell by the wayside.

The Visitors devoted most of their attention to detailed questions of discipline, administration, and curriculum. They were frankly partisans of the new learning, and hostile to scholasticism. But the Edwardian code was soon superseded by the Marian reaction, and the Visitors' chief claim to a permanent effect on the University is the destruction which they instigated and encouraged in the University Library and the college chapels. Duke Humphrey's noble collection of books was dispersed or destroyed: the Library was left empty, and even the bookshelves were sold. College libraries suffered less drastically, but altars, statues, and the stained glass of their chapels were smashed or defaced.

At the accession of Queen Mary, Gardiner as Bishop of Winchester used his power as Visitor of New College, Magdalen and Corpus to purge those colleges of Protestants. Cardinal Pole as Archbishop of Canterbury and Chancellor of both universities ordered a new Visitation in 1556. Preoccupied with heresy, it emphasised the powers of Heads of Colleges, and the importance of the discipline of students in colleges and Halls. The Marian reaction failed to recapture the University for the Roman faith, and it defeated itself by the crowning

35 East range of the Great Quadrangle (1525–9). Christ Church

tragedy of the condemnation and burning of Ridley, Latimer and Cranmer. It was not merely the burning but the public humiliation and degradation to which they were subjected that condemned the Roman reaction. As if to make the proceedings still more macabre, Cranmer was thanked by the examiners for taking part in the disputation of a candidate for the Doctorate of Divinity, the day before he was condemned as a heretic.

TRINITY, ST JOHN'S, JESUS

In those troublous times two new colleges were founded in the year 1555 – Trinity and St John's. It is significant of the rapid transition of England from the medieval order that both founders were laymen, and that their colleges were built on the sites of dissolved monastic houses. Yet both founders were conservative and catholic in their outlook and aims, and were in favour at court under the Marian régime. Sir Thomas Pope, founder of Trinity College, was doubly connected with the dissolution of the monasteries. He was a successful Tudor official, who was Treasurer of the Court of Augmentations, the new financial department created by Cromwell to handle the proceeds of the dissolution of the monasteries. He was well placed to acquire property, and owned some twenty-seven manors in Oxfordshire. In 1555 he bought the site of the dissolved monastic Durham College of the northern province of the Benedictines, and in the same year procured letters patent from Philip and Mary for his foundation. In the following year he delivered his statutes, which followed the lines laid down by Corpus and Brasenose. There were to be twelve Fellows, eight scholars, and not more than twenty commoners. Two Readers were to supervise studies, and college lectures were to replace university lectures as 'the ordinary lectures of the Regent Masters' were becoming useless.

Sir Thomas White, the founder of St John's, was a rich tailor of the City of London, who backed Mary's accession to the throne against Lady Jane Grey. He became a Knight and Lord Mayor of London at the accession of Mary, and secured London for the Queen in Wyatt's rebellion. In 1554 he bought from Christ Church the site of the dissolved monastic house of the Cistercians, and in 1555 he obtained a royal licence to found his College of St John the Baptist, with a President and fifty Fellows. He desired his college to defend the catholic faith against the Lutherans. There were to be three Readers in Greek, Logic and Rhetoric, preferably to be appointed from the Fellows, to lecture daily. Shortly before his death in 1567, the founder provided for forty-three poor scholars, the majority to be chosen by the Company of Merchant Taylors. Not more than sixteen commoners were to be admitted.

Both these colleges had a difficult start. They were immediately faced with the awkward adjustment from the Marian to the Elizabethan régime: and their original endowments, in neither case exceeding £250 per annum, were inadequate to realise the founder's designs.

Jesus College has the distinction of being the sole Oxford college founded in the reign of Queen Elizabeth. In 1571 Dr Hugh Price obtained letters patent for a college of a Principal, eight Fellows and eight scholars, and bought the site and buildings of White Hall. But it was many years before the college acquired adequate revenues for building and stipends, and it was not till 1622 that its statutes, modelled on those of Brasenose, were fixed. The founder was a Welshman, but neither he nor the statutes gave preference to the Welsh. The orientation of the college towards Wales developed with later benefactions.

36 St John the Baptist and St Mary Magdalen; carved panel (1541) on the west wall of the hall. Magdalen College

Holinshed begins his chronicle of the reign of Queen Elizabeth with these words: 'After all the tempestuous and blustering windy weather of Queen Mary was overthrown, the darksome cloud of discomfort dispersed, the palpable fogs and misery consumed, and the dashing showers of persecution overpast; it pleased God to send England a calm and quiet season, a clear and lovely sunshine, a quiet rest from former broils of a turbulent estate, and a world of blessings from good Queen Elizabeth.' One of the best educated monarchs in English history, Queen Elizabeth was also immune from the religious and doctrinal passions of the age. It was clear that public opinion, after the Marian persecution, would not tolerate a continued connection with Rome, and her aim was to damp down the fires of religious passion, and obtain a religious settlement as comprehensive and broadly-based as possible. In this she was temporarily successful, despite the increasing embarrassments and dangers caused both by the Jesuit fifth-column after the Bull of Excommunication in 1570, and by the rising tide of Puritanism.

William Allen, Fellow of Oriel, Edmund Campion, Fellow of St John's, and Robert Parsons, Fellow of Balliol, left Oxford for the Continent to lead the Romanist and Jesuit Crusade to regain England for Rome. But it is only roughly true that Oxford specialised in Romanism, and Cambridge in Puritanism. The Heads of Magdalen, Christ Church and Corpus were strongly Puritan, and Dean Sampson of Christ Church was eventually deprived for contumaciously refusing to wear a surplice.

With the experience of the explosive forces generated in the universities in the first half of the century, Elizabeth and her government kept a watchful and maternal eye on the universities. Characteristically, the Queen did not spend her money on the universities; but she took the trouble to gain their loyalty. In 1566 and in 1592, her visits to Oxford each lasted a week. The colleges groaned at the expense of entertaining the court, but the Queen's genuine interest in learning, her tact, her unique and lonely dignity as the symbol of the nation's unity and safety, aroused affection and enthusiasm. Unity was the theme of her last speech in Christ Church; pride, affection, and a note of anxiety for the future, in her parting words at Shotover: 'Farewell, dear Oxford, God bless thee! God bless thee and increase thy sons in numbers, holiness, and virtue'.

After the final breach with Rome, the universities had been legally and theoretically exposed to the terrifying Tudor autocracy. The Visitation of 1559 had been cautious and moderate, and confined itself to purging the obvious Romanists; about half the Heads of colleges, but only a minority of Fellows, were removed. In 1571 the status and privileges of the universities were confirmed and defined by Act of Parliament. But governmental control was shrewdly and subtly exercised by indirect rule, Sir William Cecil becoming Chancellor of Cambridge and Leicester Chancellor of Oxford. Leicester resumed the right to nominate the Vice-Chancellor, and letters of recommendation from the court were freely used to influence the election of Heads and Fellows of colleges. It was in line with government policy to encourage an oligarchy of Heads of colleges, at the expense of the Congregation of Regent Masters. At Cambridge this was effected by a violent constitutional revolution in 1570.

At Oxford the change came about more smoothly and unobtrusively, with Leicester encouraging the Heads of colleges to meet and prepare beforehand the business of Congregation. 'Whoe will not think it reasonable,' asked Leicester, 'that before the Convocation, the Vice-Chancellor, Doctors, Heads and Proctors should consult of such things as are fittest to be moved therein?' Later King Charles I, at the instance of Laud, was to direct that there should

37 Wadham College Hall (1610–13)
38 *(overleaf)* Vault of the Great Staircase (c. 1640). Christ Church

be a weekly meeting of the Conventus Praefectorum, the Heads of colleges and Halls, to conduct the business of the University and prepare measures to be presented to Convocation.

The new position of Heads of colleges also owed something to a curious, almost accidental result of the Reformation. The medieval statutes of colleges did not expressly forbid Heads of colleges to marry, as they did in the case of Fellows. By following the example of the Elizabethan bishops and marrying, they formed themselves into a separate caste, less closely in contact with the Fellows of their colleges.

SOCIAL AND EDUCATIONAL CHANGE

The second half of the sixteenth century was a critical turning-point for the University. With the increasing secularisation of the professions and of education the University might have been left as a clerical backwater, a mere seminary for the training of priests. The bishops, pre-occupied with the problem of the supply and education of parochial clergy, would have welcomed such a development. Bishop Latimer complained in 1549 that 'there are none but great men's sons in Colleges and their fathers look not to have them preachers'. The Inns of Court were increasing competitors to the universities in higher education. Educational reformers like Sir Humphrey Gilbert wanted new academies, specially designed for the education of the nobility. He pointed out that thereby the universities 'shall better suffice to relieve poor scholars, where now the growth of nobility and gentlemen, taking up their scholarships and Fellowships, do disappoint the poor of their livings and advancements'.

The educational theorists had already been left behind. From the beginning of the Elizabethan age, the nobility and gentry were moving into the universities in an increasing flood. The university matriculation register started in 1565, although far from complete until the end of the seventeenth century, indicates a significant trend. Entrants to the University were classified as noble, gentry, or plebeian according to a varying scale of fees. Not only was the total number of entrants rising sharply, but also the proportion of entrants who were noble or gentry. The constant complaints and regulations about extravagant dress and behaviour reflect this change in social composition. Allowing for the considerable number who escaped registration, it appears that between 1570 and 1590, nearly 400 were entering Oxford yearly: after a slight fall in the last years of Elizabeth, the entry climbed steadily to a peak of nearly 600 in the decade 1630-40. Cambridge follows a similar pattern.

At the same time, the complaints that nobles and gentry were monopolising the universities were exaggerated. Certainly the change in the social composition of the University from the medieval university was marked, but the plebs were maintaining a substantial slice – about half – in the increased intake, and in the increased number of scholarships; they were also able to supplement their maintenance as servitors or sizars to the nobles and gentry.

This evolution of the University follows and reflects the evolution of Tudor society. The control of local government by the gentry as Justices of the Peace, which is so marked a feature of Tudor government, meant that the gentry now needed higher education to carry out their duties and maintain their prestige as a governing-class, even if they did not aim at entering a profession. The proportion of Members of the House of Commons who were graduates of Oxford and Cambridge was rising sharply. In 1563, 110 M.P.s, 26 per cent of the total, were graduates of Oxford or Cambridge; in 1640–2, 276, or half the total, were graduates.

The humanist movement in the universities convinced the upper classes, and the rising middle class aspiring to become gentry, that virtue, wisdom and good manners were to be obtained through higher education. The value placed on education by all levels of Tudor society above that of the labouring poor is shown by the immense growth of grammar schools as well as of private schools, which by the end of the century had more than made good the damage and dislocation of the Reformation.

The opening of the colleges to fee-paying commoners, the development of a college tutorial system, the tightening of discipline within the colleges, made them attractive to upper-class parents. Young gentlemen in their teens were less exposed to temptations in Oxford than in the rough and tumble of the Inns of Court in London. Colleges equally welcomed the financial support from fee-paying commoners. Fellows of colleges who could no longer, since the Reformation, look to a career in a royal civil service monopolised by clerics, could now look to a career as college tutors, supplementing their fellowship stipends with pupils' fees.

The college tutorial system was flexible enough to be adapted to the needs of the noble and gentry. The educational process of the University was rapidly passing from the obsolescent lectures of the Regent Masters into the hands of the college tutors, who were ready to adjust their teaching to the needs of young men who might be spending a year or two at the University before proceeding to the Inns of Court without aiming at a degree. If it is true of the medieval university that the formal university statutes are an inadequate guide to the intellectual life of the University, it is particularly true of the Elizabethan period. Even today the observer would get rather an odd idea of the University if he looked only at the university statutes.

Much would depend on the individual tutor or college, but occasional references to subjects of disputation suggest that rhetoric, modern history, classics, even mathematics and natural science, were gaining ground against the traditional scholastic logic. But at the end of the sixteenth century, classical humanism still held the field: the real intellectual revolution initiated by Galileo belongs to the seventeenth century. When Galileo's *Siderius Nuncius* reached England in 1611 the poet John Donne could write:

> And new Philosophy calls all in doubt,
> The Element of fire is quite put out;
> The Sun is lost, and th' earth, and no man's wit
> Can well direct him where to looke for it.

40 Portrait of Queen Elizabeth I (1590). Jesus College

4 Laud and the Civil War

THOMAS BODLEY

The Elizabethan age at Oxford was crowned by Sir Thomas Bodley's restoration of the University Library, a work which was to make his name the best known of all Oxford's bene-factors. A graduate of Magdalen College, and a Junior Fellow of Merton, he lectured on Greek and became expert in Hebrew. He served as Proctor in 1569, and in 1576 obtained leave from his college to travel. Through his knowledge of foreign languages he became drawn into a diplomatic career, acting as the Queen's confidential envoy to Denmark, and to King Henry III of France. From 1589–96, when he retired to Oxford, he was the Queen's ambassador in the key post of the Netherlands.

In 1598 the University accepted his offer to restore the Library, and until his death in 1613 he actively supervised the work – and also the librarian. He was shocked when the librarian announced his intention to marry, and wrote that he had hoped his librarian was 'alienissimus from any such cogitation'. Besides his own extensive book-buying, he made use of his 'great store of honourable friends' to encourage gifts of books to the library. By 1602, the library was reopened with 2,000 books; the first printed catalogue in 1605 contained 6,000 items. Bodley was knighted by King James I, who twice visited the library in 1605 and 1614. King James greatly enjoyed taking part in a disputation about the evils of tobacco, and declared that 'if I was not a King I would be an Oxford man'.

In 1610 Bodley negotiated an agreement with the Stationers' Company that they should give the Library a copy of every book they printed. When confirmed by Star Chamber decree in 1637, and by parliamentary statute under Charles II, this agreement made the Bodleian Library the first national library in England. By his will Bodley ensured the completion of his magnif-icent plan for the Library; not only by leaving for it the bulk of his estate, but by laying down the blueprint for the great quadrangle of new Schools, with a third storey giving 'a very large supplement for the stowage of Bookes'. He also wanted 'some beautifull enlargement' of the Library at the west end towards Exeter College. In accordance with his plans, the quadrangle was built between 1613 and 1624, and the western end, which was to house Selden's bequest of books, with a new Convocation House beneath it, was built between 1634 and 1636.

The origins of the University Press are also Elizabethan. With the encouragement of Leicester as Chancellor, licence was given to Joseph Barnes in 1586 to act as Printer to the University, at his own financial liability. In 1632 Laud procured letters patent which allowed the University to have three printers with the right to print all kinds of books not publicly forbidden.

The religious and constitutional quarrels of the age of James I and Charles I, the ineffectual fussiness of Stuart government, culminating in Laud's ill-advised efforts to assert his metropolitan rights of Visitation as Archbishop, have obscured the progress of education and learning in this period. The educational boom, not only in numbers but in new benefactions and foundations, continued till the eve of the Civil War.

Sir Henry Savile, founder of the Savilian Professorships of Geometry and Astronomy in 1619, had been elected a Fellow of Merton in 1565, and on becoming Regent Master, lectured on the *Almagest* of Ptolemy, establishing his reputation as a mathematician and Greek scholar. His appointment as tutor in Greek to the Queen had led quickly to his election as Warden of Merton in 1585. In 1596, he persuaded the Queen to appoint him Provost of Eton, dispensing him from the statutory requirement of priest's orders, and he continued to hold the Wardenship of Merton in plurality. As a colleague at Merton, Savile was a close friend of Bodley, and helped him with the restoration of the University Library. In 1618 Sir William Sedley endowed in his will a Professorship of Natural Philosophy; in 1621 Thomas White founded a Chair in Moral Philosophy: in 1622 William Camden, the great antiquary, a Chair in History, and his friend William Heather a Chair in Music. In 1621 Lord Danvers leased the former Jews' Cemetery opposite Magdalen for a 'Physic' (or botanic) Garden.

WADHAM AND PEMBROKE

Two new colleges were founded in the Jacobean and Caroline period – Wadham and Pembroke. Nicholas Wadham, a rich and childless Somerset landowner, planned to found a college. Upon his death in 1609 his intentions were carried out by his widow Dorothy Wadham. In that year the site of the former Augustinian friary was bought, and the new college buildings were completed at a cost of £12,000 provided by Dorothy Wadham from her life-interest in her husband's estate. Though the original statutes followed the lines of New College and Corpus, they included some new features. The Warden was to be unmarried and a Doctor of Divinity, but the Fellows were not required to be in orders. They might travel abroad, but they must vacate their fellowship after eighteen years from their mastership. Though small in numbers and endowment in its first decade, the college was destined to play a notable part under the Commonwealth in the origins of the Royal Society.

Pembroke College was created by the promotion of the existing Broadgates Hall. The last Principal of Broadgates Hall, Dr Clayton, became the first Master of Pembroke College in 1624: the college received its name from the Chancellor, the Earl of Pembroke, but the initiative in the foundation came from the Mayor and Corporation of Abingdon, who petitioned the King to turn Broadgates Hall into a college, allotting to it the benefactions of Thomas Tesdale and Rev. Richard Wightwick, which gave preference to Fellows and Scholars from Abingdon School. Tesdale had left £5,000 in trust at his death in 1610, and although some Tesdale scholars had already gone to Balliol, the Balliol connection had not been formally concluded. The statutes of 1628 specifically mention gentlemen commoners who were entitled to dine at the same table as the Master and Bachelors, and also servitors – students who paid their way by menial tasks. The financial arrangements were peculiar, as the college as such at first received no endowments: the income of the Tesdale and Wightwick benefactions went to individual Fellows and Scholars. The Master's emoluments remained those of a Principal of a Hall, derived from fees and rents of rooms.

42 Central feature of the west range of Canterbury Quadrangle
(1632–6) with statue of Queen Henrietta Maria. St John's College

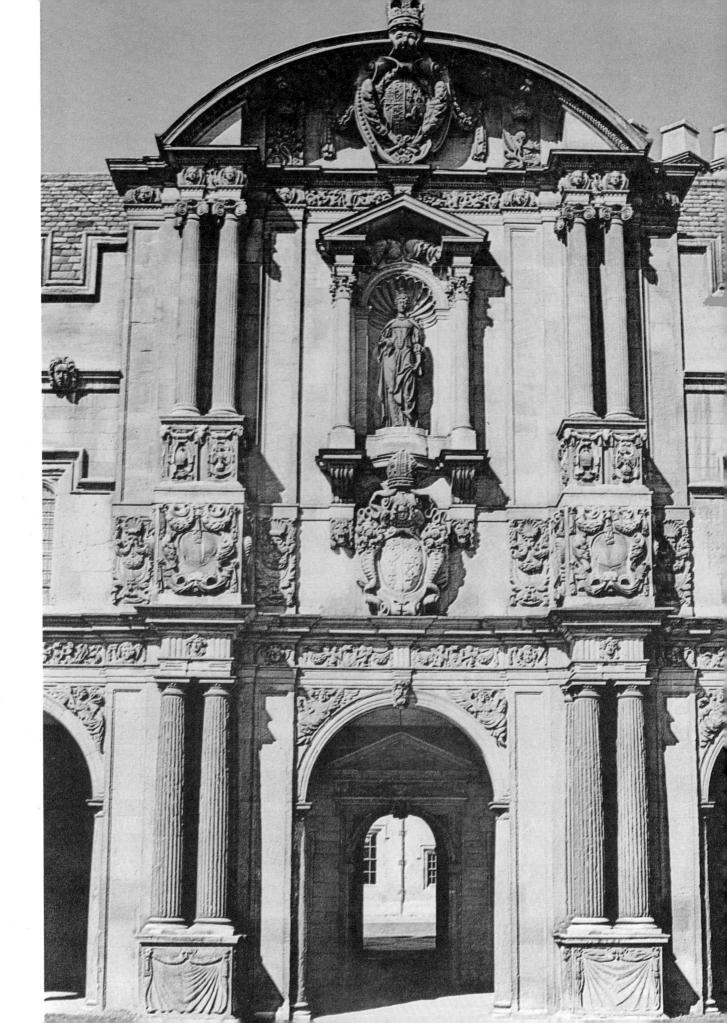

In 1630 William Laud succeeded the Earl of Pembroke as Chancellor of the University. A scholar and then Fellow of St John's, he first became known to the Court as chaplain to the Earl of Devonshire. He was President of St John's from 1611 to 1621, then successively Bishop of St David's, 1621, Bishop of Bath and Wells, 1626, Bishop of London in 1628 and Archbishop of Canterbury in 1633.

Under Laud, his predecessor and tutor Buckeridge, and his great friend Juxon, who succeeded him as President, St John's had become a stronghold of the Arminian faction. When he became Chancellor of the University and Archbishop, Laud was determined that this movement should be extended to the whole University, and the whole Church. Laud was a dangerous person in politics, a humourless, dedicated man with a mission, who never wavered in his opinions or doubted his own judgment. While he was a Fellow of St John's, his sermons had made him notorious in the University as 'a busy and pragmatical person ... at least very popishly inclined'.

The Arminian faction was so named from Arminius, the Dutch theologian who attacked the dominant Calvinist dogma of predestination. Beneath these obscure doctrinal debates lay a vital struggle for power. Laud conceived his mission to be a counter-reformation in the Church without a return to Rome. The Roman principles of episcopal and priestly authority, and orthodoxy outwardly expressed in ordered ritual were to be reasserted in the English church. The Elizabethan principle of comprehension and ambiguity was no longer acceptable. To the men of the early seventeenth century religious toleration was regarded not as a virtue but as a vice. Nor was it practicable, as religious principles were also political claims. As Wentworth wrote to Laud about the Puritans, 'These men do but begin with the Church that they might have free access to the State.'

The policy of 'Thorough' pressed by Wentworth and Laud between 1629 and 1640 was logical, but it was doomed to failure. Faced with a court suspected of popery, a divided aristocracy, a powerful, educated and politically conscious gentry and middle class, they had not the money nor the centralised administrative machinery, nor the armed force to maintain it. The eleven years' effort so tightened the tensions in Church and State that an explosion inevitably followed. Laud was impeached in 1641 and executed by the rump of the Long Parliament in 1645: at the Restoration his bones were removed to his College of St John's.

Laud's tenure of the Chancellorship of the University was not likely therefore to be uneventful. Materially and aesthetically he was a great benefactor of the University. He built at his own expense the lovely Canterbury Quadrangle of St John's, with its statues of King Charles I and Queen Henrietta Maria. He promoted the building of the porch of the University church with its baroque statue of the Virgin, which profoundly shocked his Puritan opponents. It was through his influence that the Earl of Pembroke purchased and gave to the Bodleian the great Barocci Collection of 242 Greek MSS; and that Sir Kenelm Digby gave St John's his collection of Arabic books, and to the Bodleian the library bequeathed to him by his tutor, Dr Thomas Allen, Master of Gloucester Hall, the most renowned mathematician of his day. In 1635 Laud founded a Chair of Arabic, expressly with the object of gaining for Oxford the services of the great scholar Edward Pococke.

Laud's love of Oxford was genuine but his embrace was stifling. His first action as Chancellor was to demand a weekly report from the Vice-Chancellor. One of Laud's obsessions was the long hair of fashionable undergraduates, and the Vice-Chancellor was goaded into issuing

43 *The Temptation of Adam and Eve;* stained-glass window (1641) by
Abraham van Linge. University College Chapel

edicts on this subject. In 1631 the Calvinist opposition to Laud, now in a minority, was silenced by prompt and drastic action. Hodges of Exeter College, Fox of Magdalen Hall, and Thorne of Balliol, who preached sermons against Laud's doctrines, were summoned by the Vice-Chancellor and appealed to Convocation. The Vice-Chancellor referred the matter to the King, and as a result the three Fellows were deprived and banished; the Proctors who had allowed the appeal to Convocation were compelled to resign; Dr Prideaux, the Calvinist Professor of Divinity, and Dr Wilkinson, Principal of Magdalen Hall, were reprimanded.

In 1636 Laud's stamp on Oxford was sealed by the promulgation of the Laudian statutes. Convocation obsequiously addressed Laud as 'our father, leader, angel, archangel'. Laud's connection with the statutes is like Napoleon's in relation to the *Code Civil;* he was the driving force which brought to completion a long-delayed project. The work was in the hands of a Committee, which included Dr James, Bodley's Librarian, and Brian Twyne, the antiquary. Their job was to compile and modify the existing statutes, incorporating the reform of the last hundred years. Laud himself was particularly interested in the elaboration of the examination statutes. The Regent Masters were still to examine *viva voce*, by disputation, but the content was becoming more modern. Laud wrote that he was pleased to hear that the examiners were 'asking fundamental questions, not propounding studied subtleties to gravel and discourage young students'. Nevertheless, the Laudian codification, like the Napoleonic Code, was bound to have the effect of freezing development and inhibiting change.

It is a startling indication of the extent to which Tudor and Stuart royal interference in the University had undermined its independence that nobody at the time knew whether the statutes rested on the authority of Convocation or of the King. Laud himself had little use for autonomy or privileges; as Visitor of All Souls he imposed without hesitation his own nominee to a fellowship. In 1635 Laud revived Arundel's claim to visit the universities as Archbishop and Metropolitan, mainly to assert his authority in Cambridge where he had no other standing. The universities jointly protested that they were subject only to royal visitation; Laud insisted on his rights as Archbishop, and was upheld by the King at a Hampton Court conference in 1636. Laud drew up an *aide memoire* on the 'common disorders' which required his attention at Cambridge. Fortunately the Laudian régime collapsed before it could drain the universities of life and independence.

OXFORD IN THE CIVIL WAR

While few regretted the fall of Laud, the prospect of civil war was a different matter. The Vice-Chancellor of Cambridge, addressing the University in July 1641, said, 'We will hang our harps on the willows and now at length bid a long farewell to learning ...' 'Tis now the twelfth hour alike of the Muses and the Graces.' At Oxford, the town was for Parliament, the University for the King. In July 1642, the King asked for a loan from the University, and £10,000 was sent from the University and the colleges. Some three hundred university volunteers started drilling. In September, Lord Saye and Sele, the local Parliamentarian leader, occupied Oxford for a short time, but after the victory of Edgehill in October King Charles I entered Oxford, and having failed to take London, proceeded to make Oxford the royalist headquarters for the remainder of the war. By flooding its surrounding meadows, the City was made suitable for defence.

From 1642 to 1646 the academic life of the University was in suspense. The undergraduates flocked mainly to the royalist army, and new entrants dwindled to a handful. The colleges

THOMAS SACKVILLUS DORSET. COMES,
SUMMUS ANGLIÆ THESAURAR. ET
HUJUS ACAD. CANCELLAR.
THOMÆ BODLEJO EQUITI AURATO
BIBLIOTHECAM HANC INSTITUIT
RIS CAUSA P.P.

housed courtiers and their ladies, politicians and officers, as commensales, who did not often pay their bills. College rents were difficult to collect. In June 1643 the King asked the colleges to send all their silver plate to be melted in the Royal Mint, now established in Oxford. Compensation was to be paid at a standard rate 'as soon as God shall enable us'. But this pledge was not redeemed at the Restoration. Exeter College pleaded that it would be contrary to their statutes to surrender their plate: St John's offered to compound by a money contribution. Both were forced to comply. Corpus Christi College, whether by concealment or skilful negotiation, managed to retain a substantial quantity of their pre-Reformation silver.

In May 1645 Fairfax began the investment of Oxford, but lifted the siege in June to begin the campaign which ended in the King's defeat at Naseby. In April 1646 the final siege began. The King escaped in disguise from Oxford on 27 April leaving his Council power to negotiate, and Fairfax summoned the garrison to surrender; 'I verie much desire the preservation of that place (so famous for learning) from ruine, which inevitably is like to fall upon it except you concur.' Fairfax had to manage his own officers who were confident that Oxford could be taken by assault, while the Council had to face the wrath of the royalist officers who wished to prolong the defence. But on 20 June the Articles of Surrender were signed. On entering the City, Fairfax' first action was to put a guard to protect the Bodleian Library. He later left to the Library an important collection of books. Oxford's debt to Fairfax, a Cambridge man from St John's College, is indeed very great.

OXFORD UNDER THE COMMONWEALTH

The University which had enthusiastically supported the King's cause, almost to its last shilling, now lay at the mercy of the victors. Yet the retribution was comparatively light, and the recovery surprisingly rapid. To a considerable extent the asperities of the Civil War were softened by the fact that so many members of the Long Parliament, including Cromwell himself, were graduates of Oxford and Cambridge. Extremists denounced the universities as 'nurseries of wickedness, the nests of mutton-tuggers, the dens of formal droanes'. But the leaders were wiser, and showed remarkable patience with the obstruction to parliamentary visitation maintained by royalist Heads of colleges. Selden, an Oxford graduate from Hart Hall, and one of the most respected and influential men on the Parliament side, warned of the danger that they might 'destroy rather than reform one of ye most famous and learned companyes of men that ever was visible in ye Christian world'. In 1651 Cromwell became a respected Chancellor of the University.

In May 1647 Parliament appointed a Visitatorial Commission, headed by Sir Nathaniel Brent, Warden of Merton, and a standing committee to receive reports and to hear appeals. For a year the University, led by the Vice-Chancellor, Samuel Fell, Dean of Christ Church, frustrated the Visitors by passive resistance, till the London Committee was forced to the point of deposing the Vice-Chancellor and Proctors, and appointing Reynolds as Vice-Chancellor in place of Fell. Members of colleges were required to take the 'Negative Oath' abjuring the royal cause. In 1649 the London Committee imposed the 'Engagement' to be faithful to a Commonwealth as established without a King or House of Lords. Six Heads submitted, and ten were deprived and replaced. In view of the predominantly royalist and Arminian composition of the colleges, the expulsion of Fellows was on a much greater scale than in the Reformation. The Board of Visitors, with several changes of membership, remained in being till 1658, though some freedom of election to fellowships was restored by 1651. The London Committee frequently intervened to make partisan appointments to fellowships.

Yet the Visitors appointed some Heads of colleges who were by any standards distinguished. Owen at Christ Church, and Conant of Exeter who succeeded him as Vice-Chancellor in 1657, were powerful administrators and champions of the University, as well as distinguished scholars. By 1658 the admissions and matriculation were almost restored to the pre-war level. Antony Wood, the antiquary and historian of the University who was an undergraduate at Merton in the Civil War and royalist in sympathy, records of Conant that 'though the times that then were were very dangerous and ticklish, and the mouths of the men in power began to water upon the Colleges and the revenues thereunto belonging yet the Doctor stoutly defended his post, maintaining the rights and liberties of the universities, and kept all in peace and quiet'.

BEGINNINGS OF THE ROYAL SOCIETY

The appointment of Wilkins, Warden of Wadham, Goddard, Warden of Merton, Petty, Vice-Principal of Brasenose, and the two new Savilian Professors, Wallis and Seth Ward, distinguished mathematicians from Cambridge, gave a powerful impetus to the development of science in Oxford.

It is clear that the pioneering work in the scientific revolution had started outside the universities. The Elizabethan and Laudian evolution of the universities as pillars of the Establishment for the 'virtuous training of youth' had largely obscured and depressed their original medieval function of advancing the frontiers of knowledge. The most advanced mathematicians of the Elizabethan and Jacobean age, Dee, Recorde, Harriot, Gilbert, Napier, Oughtred, did not hold university posts. Wallis, as an undergraduate at Emmanuel College, Cambridge, complained that he had to go to Oughtred, who had left King's College, Cambridge, for a country parsonage, to learn mathematics. 'For Mathematics, at that time with us, was scarce looked upon as Academical Studies, but rather Mechanical. The study of Mathematics was at that time more cultivated in London than in the Universities.'

Francis Bacon and Thomas Hobbes, the two great publicists of the scientific revolution, castigated the universities for their neglect of science. Bacon wrote that 'destined for the abode of learned men and the improvement of learning, everything is found to be opposed to the sciences'. They were full of 'cobwebs of learning ... of no substance or profit'. Hobbes wrote in *Leviathan* 'That wee have of Geometry which is the Mother of all Naturall Science, wee are not indebted for it to the Schools'. William Harvey, the discoverer of the circulation of the blood, had to go to Padua to learn the latest medical discoveries.

In Elizabethan London the needs of navigation and exploration were creating a demand for mathematics. In 1596 Sir Thomas Gresham founded Gresham College in London, leaving in his will his house in the City and an endowment for seven professors, who were to lecture publicly in the English tongue. In addition to the traditional arts subjects of divinity, law, rhetoric and music, there were to be professors in physic, geometry, and astronomy. The first professors were chosen from Oxford and Cambridge, which helped to denude the universities of their more enterprising scholars, though Henry Briggs, the first Professor of Geometry, who was associated with Napier in the development of logarithms, went on to Oxford to succeed Sir Henry Savile in the Savilian Chair. Later on Goddard, Wren and Hooke were Gresham Professors.

In the first half of the seventeenth century, therefore, a handful of scientific pioneers were struggling against official conservatism. Bodley and Savile tried to encourage mathematics, but the Laudian statutes reasserted Aristotle 'whose authority is supreme'. The reformers got their chance during the Interregnum, only to be uprooted by the Restoration. In 1679 Hobbes remarked that 'Natural Philosophy has removed from the Universities to Gresham College'.

John Wilkins, who became Warden of Wadham in 1648 and Master of Trinity, Cambridge, in 1659, had in 1640 written a *Discourse concerning a New Planet*, in which he defended the Copernican theory and denied any conflict between religion and scientific inquiry. He and Jonathan Goddard had been the active conveners of the group interested in 'experimental philosophy' which first met in London in 1645, at Gresham College or Goddard's lodgings. With Wilkins and Goddard, Wallis, Seth Ward and Petty installed at Oxford, the main group gravitated there in 1649. Wilkins persuaded Robert Boyle to settle in Oxford in 1654. Christopher Wren, who took his M.A. at Wadham in 1653, and Robert Hooke of Christ Church were the brilliant young men of the group. Boyle, Hooke and Wallis were second only to Newton as scientists of originality and genius. Wallis developed the calculus. Boyle's atmospheric experiments laid the foundations for the development of the steam engine. William Petty, who was appointed Professor of Anatomy in 1651, was sent by Cromwell to survey Ireland, and developed the science of 'Political Arithmetic' or statistics. The eminent anatomists Thomas Willis and Richard Lower were practising physicians in Oxford. For a brief period Oxford was the most active and exciting centre of scientific research in Europe. Though there were regular meetings of 'the Clubbe' at Oxford, it was not till 1660 that a London meeting launched the Royal Society, which was housed in Gresham College until 1710. As a result of the Restoration, Wilkins, Goddard and Petty had been deprived of their university posts. But Dr Wallis records that 'Dr. Wilkins and Dr. Goddard, through all these changes, continued those meetings (and had a great influence on them) from the first original till the days of their death'. Moreover, by his will Wilkins was the first substantial benefactor of the Royal Society.

Wilkins and Goddard had both graduated from Magdalen Hall. So had Thomas Hobbes, the *enfant terrible* of the scientific and rationalist movement, whose views were so shocking that he could not be admitted to the Royal Society. Moreover, Magdalen Hall under its Principal, John Wilkinson, who had been censured in 1631 for his attack on Laud, had become an anti-Laudian stronghold. Wilkins had been chaplain to Lord Saye and Sele and had married Cromwell's sister. Goddard was Cromwell's chief army physician. Wallis was a Calvinist, educated at Emmanuel, the most Puritan college in Cambridge. Robert Boyle was a fervent Christian, inclining to Puritanism, all his life, and wrote as much on theology as on science.

Sprat, writing the official history of the Royal Society under the Restoration, was not anxious to emphasise the association between the origins of the Royal Society and the Commonwealth. In its early days the Society was afraid that its activities would expose it to charges of infidelity and atheism. At the opening of the Sheldonian Theatre in 1669, the preacher, with remarkable tactlessness considering that the architect of the Sheldonian was Christopher Wren, F.R.S., inveighed against 'Cromwell, fanatics, the Royal Society and new philosophy'. In 1691 Halley was passed over for the Savilian Chair because of rumours that he was an atheist. By the end of the seventeenth century, science had become accepted and reputable. In the first half of the century the Copernican theory was still a hypothesis: by the end of it the Newtonian cosmology had triumphed. This was due not only to the dazzling achievements of Galileo and Newton, but to the success of the Royal Society in securing the patronage of Charles II, and in averting a clash between science and religion by parading the religious respectability of its members.

Edward Hyde, Earl of Clarendon, graduate of Magdalen Hall, Oxford, the most moderate of Charles I's advisers, the architect of the Restoration, and Chancellor of the University in the first decade of Charles II's reign after 1660, acknowledged in his *History of the Great Rebellion* that the Interregnum had 'yielded a harvest of extraordinary good and sound knowledge in all parts of learning: and many who were wickedly introduced applied themselves to the study of good learning and the practice of virtue: so that when it pleased God to bring the King back to his throne, he found that University abounding in excellent learning, and devoted to duty and obedience, little inferior to what it was before its desolation'.

46 Illustrations to the Old and New Testaments; stained-glass by
Bernard van Linge (1631). Lincoln College Chapel

Sicut Moses exaltauit serpent

Sicut enim fuit Ionas in uentre cet ribus

47 Statue of the Virgin and Child (1637) on the south porch of the
Church of St Mary the Virgin

5 The Oxford of Church and King

The eighteenth century notoriously shares with the fifteenth the melancholy distinction of being the worst period of decline and stagnation in the University's history. The decline was not obvious till 1715, and reached its lowest point in the middle of the eighteenth century. By 1800 there were signs of revival, paving the way for the Victorian reform of the University.

The seeds of the decline were sown at the Restoration of 1660. The royalist and Anglican establishment, restored by the 'miracle' of 1660, had sustained a bad fright from the experience of the Civil War and the Interregnum: they were determined to recapture and fortify the positions which they had so nearly lost for good and all. For them, the universities were a key-position, as the training-ground of the Church, and a potential source of subversive ideas. It was argued that the over-production of graduates in the first half of the century had been a factor in the Great Rebellion. In 1611 Lord Chancellor Ellesmere had pointed out the need for 'better livings for learned men than of more learned men for these livings, for learning without living doth but breed traitors'. The reactionary royalist Marquis of Newcastle advised Charles II that the population of the universities and the grammar schools should be cut by half.

From the Civil War onwards, contemporary comment on Oxford becomes more voluminous and richer. John Aubrey gives in his Autobiography a pleasing picture of undergraduate life at Trinity College, when he returned in 1646 after the siege: 'Here and at Middle Temple (off and on) I (for the most part) enjoyed the greatest felicity of my life (ingeniose youths, as rosebudds, imbibe the morning dew) till Dec. 1648'. The diaries of those two acidulous antiquaries Antony Wood (who died in 1695) and Thomas Hearne (who died in 1735) are lively but biased. They found it difficult to praise anybody, and their tempers were soured by the feeling that their merits were ignored by the university establishment. Antony Wood was suspected of popery, and Hearne was a non-juror and fervent Jacobite. Nicholas Amhurst who was sent down by his college, St John's, became a ferocious Whig critic and pamphleteer, in his magazine *Terrae Filius*, which ran for six months in 1721.

The Restoration Parliament demanded that the Chancellors of Oxford and Cambridge should do justice to all persons 'unjustly put out'. The Visitation of 1660 therefore aimed at reversing the purges of 1647, and making Oxford safe for Anglicanism. It was indiscriminate and partisan in its operation: it removed not only some inferior political appointments of the Commonwealth, but valuable men such as Goddard of Merton and Seth Ward (President-Elect of Trinity, Oxford). Wilkins of Wadham lost the Mastership of Trinity, Cambridge, to which he had transferred a few months before. But after more than a decade, there were not many of the pre-Commonwealth Fellows available for reinstatement, and many of the Fellows appointed in the Commonwealth were ready to conform to retain their places. The change in total was therefore much smaller than in 1647, but the result was as bad or worse. It removed good and bad together, and left undisturbed a mass of inferior Fellows intruded by the Commonwealth.

Antony Wood remarks that 'Some cavaliers that were restored by the King's commissioners were good scholars but the generality dunces'. 'As for the junior scholars trained up in the Presbyterian discipline, it cannot be imagined what ways they took to express themselves reall converts for the prelaticall party upon this change.' The net result of the purges of the Civil War and the Restoration was a serious dilution of the quality of the teaching body of the University, which may well have initiated the decline apparent in the eighteenth century. Once the vitality was lacking, the Laudian statutes and the medieval college statutes gave every excuse for inertia.

The Act of Uniformity of 1662, which perpetuated the split between the Anglican Establishment and nonconformity, not only caused a further crop of expulsions and resignations, including Conant of Exeter and Wilkinson of Magdalen Hall, but for the first time in its history cut Oxford off from an important and active section of the nation. Hence came the rise of the new Dissenting Academies.

The general relaxation of manners and morals after Puritan rule, sourly described by Wood, was stimulated by the frequent visits of Charles II's court. Already in 1661 Wood comments, 'Before the warr wee had scholars that made a thorough search in scholasticall and polemicall divinity, in humane authors, and naturall philosophy. But now scholars studie these things not more than what is just necessary to carry them through the exercises of their respective Colleges and the Universitie. Their aim is not to live as students ought to viz. temperat, abstemious and plain and grave in the apparell; but to live like gent. to keep dogs and horses, to turn their studies and coleholes into places to receive bottles, to swash it in apparell, to wear long periwigs etc.; and the theologists to ride abroad in grey coats with swords by their sides. The masters have lost their respect by being themselves scandalous and keeping company with undergraduates.' He describes the courtiers as 'rude, rough, whoremongers, vaine, empty, careless'. Stage-plays, revived to 'spite the Presbyterians', started in the yard of the King's Arms tavern in Holywell and the novelty of female players 'made the scholars mad'.

Charles II was in Oxford in 1663, in 1665 for four months to escape the plague, and in 1681 he summoned Parliament to Oxford, at the height of his struggle with Shaftesbury and the Whigs over the Popish Plot and the exclusion of James, Duke of York, from the succession. A loyal University greeted Charles with delirious enthusiasm, and it was in the House of Lords, sitting in the Geometry School in the Bodleian Quadrangle, that the King dished the Whigs by the sudden Dissolution of Parliament. In 1683 Convocation denounced 'certain pernicious books and damnable doctrines destructive to the sacred persons of princes'. Hobbes' works were among those burnt in the Schools Quadrangle. In 1684 Christ Church was compelled by government pressure to expel the philosopher John Locke from his studentship because of his close association with Shaftesbury.

JAMES II AND MAGDALEN

It was, therefore, a situation full of dramatic irony when in 1687 Oxford and Magdalen College focussed the national dilemma of Anglican Toryism betrayed by a papist King. In 1686

48 The dome of the Radcliffe Camera and the towers of All Souls College

49 *(opposite)* Cupola over the gateway (1733) with statue of Queen Caroline. The Queen's College

50 Three pound piece (obverse and reverse) and crown (obverse) of Charles I, minted in Oxford (1643–4). Heberden Coin Room, Ashmolean Museum

51 Coronation cup of Charles II (1661). Town Hall

Obadiah Walker, Master of University College, had declared himself a Catholic. In the same year Massey, a young papist, was appointed to succeed Fell as Dean of Christ Church. In March 1687, on the death of the President of Magdalen, King James II nominated by a mandatory letter Antony Farmer, a papist, to succeed him. In Tudor and Stuart Oxford, this was not a novel proceeding: it was the ineptness of the nomination and the crudeness with which it was pressed that provoked the resistance of the Fellows. Farmer's career as a student at Cambridge and a Master of Arts at Magdalen Hall and Magdalen was notorious for drunkenness and immorality. Even Judge Jeffreys thought him 'a very bad man'. The Fellows of Magdalen ignored the royal nomination, and elected Hough, one of their own number. They were summoned by the Ecclesiastical Court of High Commission, and the election was annulled.

But the Fellows had won the first round, as the nomination of Farmer was dropped, and the King nominated Samuel Parker, Bishop of Oxford. In the course of his visit to Oxford in September 1687, James II browbeat the Fellows of Magdalen and accused them of 'downright disobedience'. 'Is this your Church of England loyalty?' In October, Royal Commissioners expelled Hough and twenty-five Fellows, and the Ecclesiastical Court declared them incapable of any preferment. In January 1688, fourteen Magdalen Demies were expelled for demonstrating against the new papist Fellows. A fortnight before William of Orange's fleet sailed for Torbay, James in a belated panic of conciliation restored Hough and the Fellows to their college. The Magdalen battle was the first open resistance to James and the crassness and ineptitude of his handling of it explains why the 'bloodless Revolution' of 1688 was possible. It is not often that Oxford dons can seriously claim to have toppled a government and a throne.

William III was not popular in Oxford, but Anglican Toryism could rally round Queen Mary and Queen Anne, and greet with enthusiasm the Tory ascendancy of 1710–14 and the shower of preferments which court favour brought to Oxford.

In an age of lesser men, a few active and powerful Heads of colleges dominated the University. The most important were John Fell, Dean of Christ Church from 1660 to 1686, and Henry Aldrich, Dean of Christ Church from 1689 to 1710. Fell, who was expelled from his studentship at Christ Church in 1648, inherited the Laudian tradition of his father, who had been Dean of Christ Church before the Civil War. He was Vice-Chancellor in 1666–8, and again in 1669, and from 1675 was allowed to hold the Deanery with the Bishopric of Oxford in plurality. A high-minded and learned autocrat, he strove vigorously to restore Laudian discipline in an age of increasing idleness and debauchery. He was a notable patron and manager of the University Press. Hearne seldom says anything good of his contemporaries but of Henry Aldrich he writes, 'He was humble and modest to a fault, a most affable, complaisant gentleman'. A lovable and kindly tutor and Dean, he was a man of wide and varied accomplishments, not only in theology, but in music, science and architecture.

THE SHELDONIAN AND THE WREN PERIOD OF ARCHITECTURE

Like the fifteenth century, the century following 1660 is a period in Oxford of magnificent architectural achievement offsetting and contrasting with its intellectual sterility. The inspiration and stimulus of Christopher Wren engendered a whole generation of bold, original and ambitious buildings which raised Oxford to an unsurpassed peak of physical beauty, until the erosion of urban development began. Succeeding generations can only be grateful that this great expansion of building took place in a period of fine architecture when master masons and

52 Tom Tower (16th century and 1681–2). Christ Church

craftsmen of the highest quality were still available. It is apparently true, though hardly credible, that it was a master mason, Thomas Wood, who designed and built the elegant Old Ashmolean, worthy companion to the Sheldonian Theatre, between 1679 and 1683. William Townesend and his son, master masons, were largely responsible for the execution of the building of the Clarendon Building, Peckwater Quadrangle and the library at Christ Church, the front of Worcester College, Queen's College and the Radcliffe Camera. Amateurs like Dean Aldrich of Christ Church and George Clarke, Fellow of All Souls, also had a hand in designing these buildings.

We must be grateful, also, that there was not enough money to carry out the more drastic plans for rebuilding in the eighteenth century. Otherwise not only the medieval Queen's College, but the medieval buildings of All Souls, Magdalen, Worcester and Hart Hall might have disappeared.

The Sheldonian Theatre was Wren's first large-scale work, and it was largely owing to Dean Fell that he was given the chance. Fell, like his Commonwealth predecessor, Owen, was scandalised by the disorder and ribaldry of the Act ceremonies held in St Mary's Church. Gilbert Sheldon, who had succeeded Juxon as Archbishop of Canterbury in 1660 and thereafter as Chancellor of the University in 1667, held the same view, and offered to pay the whole cost of a new building and its endowment. Wren's design was completed and inaugurated in July 1669. Fell then completed the great quadrangle of Christ Church, and brought in Wren to design the gateway Tom Tower, which was completed in 1684.

Wren was commissioned to build the new open-ended quadrangle of Trinity in 1665. The new chapel was begun in 1691. It is not a Wren design, though both he and Aldrich may have helped with advice, and, in the absence of documents, it is highly probable that the woodcarving is by Grinling Gibbons, who was a friend of Wren. Aldrich designed the Peckwater Quadrangle of Christ Church which was begun in 1705.

Fell and Aldrich were also consulted in the rebuilding of the Queen's College. Sir Joseph Williamson, Fellow of Queen's, had left Oxford for Whitehall in 1660, after travelling widely on the continent in the Interregnum. He became Secretary of State 1674–9 and Pepys said of him, 'The more I know him the more I honour him'. He was a man 'with whom one might be mighty merry'. When his friend Timothy Halton became Provost of Queen's in 1679, they discussed plans for the rebuilding of the college. Provost Halton built the new library in 1693–6, paying half the cost himself. In his will of 1701 Williamson left the college £6,000 and Halton's successor in 1704, Lancaster, determined to rebuild the whole college. He sought the advice of Nicholas Hawksmoor, Wren's pupil, but the final model was his own, described by a New College Fellow as 'one of the most Majestick Pieces of Architecture in the Whole Kingdom'. The hall and chapel were built between 1714 and 1719, but the whole rebuilding was not completed till 1761.

It was Hawksmoor who designed the Clarendon Building, erected in 1711–13 to house the University Press. The Sheldonian Theatre could no longer accommodate the Press, and the new building was financed from the profits of Clarendon's *History of the Great Rebellion*.

The expansion of All Souls College was due to four remarkable Fellows of the college, George Clarke (who also contributed generously in money and advice to the building of Worcester College and designed the great library of Christ Church begun in 1717), Nathaniel Lloyd, Christopher Codrington, Governor of the West Indies and founder of Barbados College, and Blackstone, the great legal historian. George Clarke and Nathaniel Lloyd were active Tory politicians in the reign of Queen Anne, and held ministerial office.

53 Sir Christopher Wren by Edward Pierce (1673). Ashmolean Museum

55

54 Interior of Trinity College Chapel (1691–4)
55 Detail from the carving of the reredos by
    Grinling Gibbons (c. 1694). Trinity College
    Chapel

Overleaf
56 Elias Ashmole by John Riley (1683); the frame
    by Grinling Gibbons. Ashmolean Museum
57 East entrance of the Old Ashmolean Museum
    (1679–83)

PRÆMIA
HONORARIA.

58   Model for the dome of the Radcliffe Camera (c. 1740). 18, St Giles

59

59 *A View of the Theatre, Printing House &c.;*
headpiece for the *Oxford Almanack* of 1800.
Ashmolean Museum

60 Hawksmoor's model for the Radcliffe
Camera (*c.* 1735). Bodleian Library

60

61   Overdoor on the garden front of 18, St Giles (1702)

The medieval quadrangle of All Souls had always been inadequate and cramped, and from the Restoration onwards the Fellows were considering schemes for expansion. Elated by Codrington's legacy of £6,000 for a new library, the Fellows decided to rebuild the whole college, and commissioned Hawksmoor to design in the 'Gothick style'. Though Hawksmoor pleaded for 'the preservation of antient durable public buildings that are strong and useful instead of erecting new, fantasticall, perishable trash', he produced designs in 1721 for rebuilding the medieval front quadrangle. The Codrington Library and the new quadrangle were completed by 1756, and the college still hoped to complete Hawksmoor's design for the front quadrangle: fortunately their hopes were deferred till the change of taste rescued the medieval buildings.

John Radcliffe, the most fashionable court physician of Queen Anne's day, left the bulk of his fortune in trust partly for the benefit of his old college, University College, and partly for the benefit of the University. In his will of 1714, he earmarked £40,000 for a library and chose the present site. The acquisition of the site caused long delays, and the building of the library did not begin till 1737; it was completed in 1748. Hawksmoor was finally rejected as the architect of the Radcliffe Library in favour of James Gibbs; but the general plan of a drum and dome was taken over by Gibbs from Hawksmoor.

WORCESTER AND HERTFORD

In contrast with the great university buildings, the Restoration and eighteenth century brought only two new colleges, both by the promotion of existing Halls. Gloucester Hall became Worcester College in 1714, and Hart Hall became Hertford College in 1740. Their foundation gave full scope to the eighteenth-century capacity for tortuous intrigue. Benjamin Woodroffe became Principal of Gloucester Hall in 1692. He is described by Hearne as 'a learned man... but wanted judgment very much and was moreover of a strange, unsettled, whimsical temper which brought him into debt'. His first plan was to found a 'Greek College' for the education of members of the Greek Orthodox Church, for which he hoped for support from the Levant Company and the Crown. This was emphatically not a success, and the last Greek student had disappeared by 1707.

In 1696 he heard that Sir Thomas Cookes of Worcestershire was planning to give or bequeath £10,000 for the endowment of a college at Oxford. He immediately drew up plans for a Worcester College, and laid siege to Sir Thomas, who was as 'whimsical' a character as Woodroffe. Woodroffe's importunity was unsuccessful, as Sir Thomas died in 1701 without altering his will of 1696, which empowered thirty trustees to found a new college or endow an existing college or Hall. By the time the trustees met in 1707 Woodroffe had not only made many enemies in the University but was seriously in debt. A majority of the trustees voted for the endowment of Magdalen Hall, but a unanimous decision was required by the will. Woodroffe was imprisoned for debt in the Fleet prison and died in 1711. With the appointment of his successor, the situation was rapidly resolved. The Tory politicians, now in power, saw an excellent opportunity to secure an additional Tory Head of a House. The Duke of Ormonde as Chancellor nominated Richard Blechynden, who was chaplain to the local Tory magnate, Lord Harcourt, and held the Harcourt family living of Nuneham Courtenay. The trustees were induced to agree that the Cookes benefaction should go to Gloucester Hall, which became Worcester College in 1714.

Dr Richard Newton, the founder of Hertford College, also had the knack of making enemies and, according to Hearne, earned the reputation of 'being a crack-brained Man, being mad with Pride and Conceit'. In the circumstances of his time 'crack-brained' he certainly was, because he actually intended to make the college system of education a reality. In 1710 he became Principal of Hart Hall, and in 1720 he published his 'Scheme of Discipline with Statutes intended to be Established by a Royal Charter for the education of youth in Hart Hall in the University of Oxford'. Tutors appointed and dismissed by the Principal were to take charge of not more than eight undergraduates throughout their University career. Every undergraduate had to do one written piece of work each week, and read it aloud before the whole college on Saturday. Discipline, inexpensive living and freedom from debt were to be enforced on scholars and gentlemen-commoners alike.

In these aims Newton was a sort of Jowett before his time: but he lacked the subtlety and humanity of Jowett, and he was a faintly ridiculous pedant. He was flayed by Nicholas Amhurst as a 'meer tyrant'. Nevertheless his régime appealed to aristocratic as well as middle-class parents, and Hart Hall attracted a large number of gentlemen-commoners. For seventeen years Exeter College, the landlords of the Hart Hall site, backed by their Visitor, the Bishop of Exeter, blocked Newton's petition for a charter as a college, ignoring the precedent established when Magdalen Hall had, at the end of the seventeenth century, obtained judgment in the courts that Magdalen College as the landlords had no rights on the Hall other than a quit-rent. The fact that Newton had powerful Whig support, if he chose to exploit it, did not endear him to the University; the Duke of Newcastle and his brother Henry Pelham, were his former pupils and friends. Thomas Strangeways, formerly of Hart Hall, and M.P. for Dorset, was the benefactor on whom Newton relied for endowment of the college, but he died in 1726. When the new Bishop of Exeter finally dropped his opposition in 1737, and Newton got his charter in 1740, the college was launched with completely inadequate endowments. It could only run with a substantial number of fee-paying gentlemen-commoners, and by the end of the century a revitalised Christ Church was attracting the lion's share of this commodity.

In 1805, on the death of the Principal, there was only one surviving Fellow of Hertford College, who was mad enough to be quite unsuitable for the succession. It seemed to the Heads of Houses that it would be politic and convenient to allow the college to die a natural death. Numbers in the University had reached their lowest ebb, and there was no pressure on accommodation. Magdalen College welcomed the opportunity presented for their inconvenient neighbour Magdalen Hall to move and take over the site of Hertford College, and offered to pay for the repair and rebuilding of the Hertford College buildings. By a drastic but probably inevitable piece of surgery, arrangement was made in 1815 for the suppression of Hertford College, and the migration of Magdalen Hall. The move was accelerated by the collapse of part of the medieval front of Hertford 'in a cloud of dust' in 1820, and almost simultaneously a fire which destroyed much of the Magdalen Hall buildings. Between 1820 and 1822, the handsome Georgian front of the new Magdalen Hall was built in Catte Street.

THE TORY DÉBÂCLE AND THE HANOVERIAN SUCCESSION

The age of William III and Anne was one of rapid social and economic change, accelerated by the continental wars against Louis XIV, and an intense struggle for power within the parliamentary arena. Tory squires and parsons reacted violently to the challenge of the Whig alliance of great landowners and court politicians with the new commercial oligarchy and dissent. They hoped to consolidate their position by the Landed Property Qualification Act

63 *(opposite)* Ceiling of the buttery (*c.* 1730). All Souls College

64 George Frederick Handel by Louis-François Roubiliac (1761). Ashmolean Museum

for parliamentary candidates, an Act against Occasional Conformity, and a Schism Act. The quarrel between the Tory leaders and the abortive negotiations for the succession of James brought them not only to defeat in 1715, but to rout and catastrophe. Bolingbroke, Atterbury and Ormonde succeeded in branding Toryism, and Oxford Toryism especially, as dangerously Jacobite. Atterbury had been Dean of Christ Church, 1710–13, before he became Bishop of Rochester. He suggested to Bolingbroke on Anne's death that he should proclaim the accession of James III: when Bolingbroke refused he exclaimed, 'There is the best cause in Europe lost for want of spirit'. Bolingbroke and then Ormonde joined the Pretender: the University promptly elected Lord Arran, Ormonde's brother, to succeed him as Chancellor of the University. In 1722 Atterbury was prosecuted and banished for complicity in a Jacobite plot.

It was not surprising that in the years following the Jacobite 1715 rising Whig governments treated Oxford with suspicion and apprehension. A student riot in May 1715 contributed to the passing of the Riot Act, and gave the government the excuse to quarter on Oxford a regiment which was not removed for several years. Between 1717 and 1719 the government were seriously considering a Visitation of the University, but the threat was averted by the split in the Whig party, when Walpole and Townshend went into opposition in 1717. After the '45 rising the threat was renewed. Toasts continued to be drunk in Oxford which, as Gibbon put it, 'were not expressive of the most lively devotion to the House of Hanover'. In February 1748 two undergraduates were indicted for uttering treason in their cups. Whitmore of Balliol was alleged to have declared in the presence of the Proctors, 'God Damn King George and all his assistants. God Bless King James III of England.' The Vice-Chancellor was also prosecuted for condoning this offence. One of the court chaplains preached against 'the pernicious effects of an intemperate indulgence in sensual pleasures'.

In April 1748 the solemn opening of the Radcliffe Camera took the form of a Tory demonstration; the Radcliffe trustees were all Tory magnates. Dr King, Principal of St Mary Hall, the friend of Samuel Johnson and the popular leader of Jacobite Toryism in the University, delivered a defiant discourse, lamenting the days of Queen Anne 'when no Briton need blush for our national honour; when our senate was uncorrupt'.

When Cambridge elected the Duke of Newcastle as their Chancellor, sour jibes came from Oxford:

> See Granta's Senate by Inducements led
> Elects wise Newcastle for their Head
> All, or in Church or State, they now may claim
> Lawn, Furs, Posts, Pensions wait the happy Cam.

It was not till Lord North became Prime Minister in 1770 and Chancellor of Oxford in 1772 that the University was once more to enjoy court favour and preferment.

Meanwhile, under the first two Georges, the Whigs could neither control the University nor ignore it. They could not resist the temptation of exploiting the Tory association with Jacobitism, and consequently excluding all but acknowledged Whigs from preferment. Nor could they build up a sufficient Whig following in the University. Merton, Exeter and Wadham Colleges were solid Whig strongholds, but the majority of the colleges, denied court favour, remained in sullen opposition. But the structure of Hanoverian politics involved the University even more closely than in the seventeenth century. Clerical propaganda remained a potent force in electioneering. The pulpit-oratory and pamphleteering of the learned clergy were the television networks of their day. The few open parliamentary constituencies like Westminster, the City of London and the Universities were important indications of political and electoral trends, watched by governments with care and apprehension. In the House of Lords, the bishops held a vital block of votes, and as they were drawn mainly from the universities, the choice and management of the bishops was a matter of constant concern to politicians. Equally, ambitious dons were well aware that the way to preferments and the prize of a bishopric lay through court or aristocratic chaplaincies, and the major part of their energies went into cultivating political connections and combinations.

THE INFLUENCE OF OLIGARCHY

By 1727, when Walpole consolidated his power at the accession of George II, oligarchy and patronage, subtler and less crude but no less effective than the bastard feudalism of the fifteenth century, had invaded every sphere of the national life. The effect of the 1688 Revolution and of the philosophy of John Locke was to create an exaggerated respect for the absolute rights of property. In the *mores* of Georgian England an office was regarded not as a responsibility but as a freehold property, to be added to other properties, or exchanged for a better one. When William Pitt the Elder refused to take the immense perquisites of the office of Paymaster General to the Forces this quixotic gesture was regarded with astonishment. Parliamentary boroughs jealously restricted the number of voters in order to keep up the price of a vote. It was unlikely therefore that the universities, ranking among the greatest and wealthiest corporate bodies in the kingdom, should escape this invasion of oligarchy.

The medieval statutes of colleges provided a happy hunting-ground for the exploitation of privilege and patronage. The closed scholarships and fellowships designed by the founders as a means of enabling poor boys to rise, now became the exclusive property of founders' kin, counties or localities.

Scholars on the foundation automatically claimed the right to succeed to fellowships, and in due course to college livings, which enabled them to marry. Colleges now devoted money and ingenuity to acquiring advowsons to livings in order to keep up the turnover of fellowships. The average Fellow was a gentleman of leisure waiting for a living. Few Fellows were interested in teaching, or even competent to do it. The exceptional student who was interested in acquiring knowledge resorted to private tutors and coaches. Even university professorships became sinecures; lecturing obligations were ignored or handed on to deputies. In the *Wealth of Nations* Adam Smith asserted that most Oxford professors 'had given up altogether even the pretence of teaching'.

A favourite Whig prescription for breaking Tory High Church control of Oxford was the abolition of the celibacy and clerical requirements for Fellows. The Church establishment had to cling to the statutes as they stood, and fortify them by appeals to founders' intentions and oaths to maintain them, for fear that any meddling with them would end the clerical monopoly.

With the increasing stratification of classes, the nobility and gentry withdrew from the local grammar schools into the public schools of Winchester, Eton and Westminster. The eighteenth century was the hey-day of the noblemen and gentlemen-commoners. Their privileged position in the colleges was emphasised by their gold-tasselled caps and elaborate robes. James Harris, later the first Earl of Malmesbury, who went up to Merton in 1763, recalled that 'the sort of men with whom I lived were very pleasant, but very idle fellows. Our life was an imitation of High Life in London; luckily drinking was not the fashion, but what we did drink was claret, and we had our regular round of evening card parties, to the great annoyance of

67   Dr Radcliffe by Francis
      Bird (1717). University
      College
68   Christopher Codrington
      by Henry Cheere (1734).
      All Souls College Library
69   *(overleaf)* Second
      Quadrangle (1729 and
      1788–9). Oriel College

71

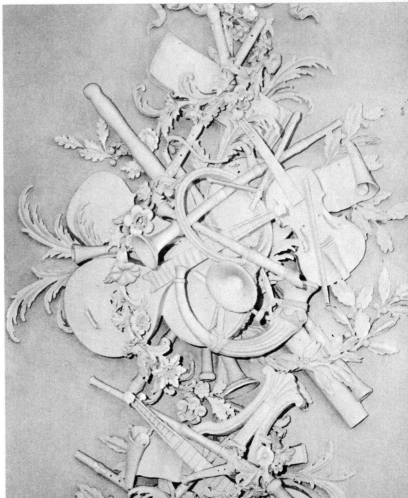

72

70 Library of the Museum of the History of
    Science
71 Dragon and infant satyr; detail of stucco in
    Jesus College Hall
72 Detail of stucco (1759) in Christ Church
    Library

our finances.' As the grammar schools with their obsolete endowments decayed, the recruits for closed scholarships declined in quality. The aristocracy now monopolised the richer benefices, canonries, prebends, deaneries; and with rare exceptions, the closed scholars and servitors could only look forward to miserable curacies worth less than £100 a year. Samuel Johnson had known the bitterness of a servitor's position as an undergraduate at Pembroke. 'The difference, Sir, between us Servitors and Gentlemen Commoners is this, that we are men of wit and no fortune, and they are men of fortune and no wit.'

The undergraduate of the eighteenth century was in no danger of being hag-ridden by examinations. The public examinations prescribed by the Laudian statutes had become a meaningless formality. It was alleged by Nicholas Amhurst that candidates chose their own examiners 'who never fail to be their old cronies and toping companions'. Disputations consisted of 'foolish syllogisms on foolish subjects, handed from generation to generation on long slips of paper'. These were called 'Strings'. The prescribed lectures for the M.A. became 'Wall-Lectures' delivered to the walls of an empty room.

Obviously a system which allowed the individual, whether don or undergraduate, to do as much or little as he liked, is open to loose and dangerous generalisation. There were conscientious, if not brilliant tutors, who lacked the follies or vices to attract the attention of the satirist. Of his tutor at Pembroke, Johnson remarked 'Whenever a young man becomes Jorden's pupil, he becomes his son.' The notorious disappointment of a Gibbon and a Bentham is balanced by the experience of Charles James Fox. In a rare fit of parental responsibility his father decided in 1764 to separate him from his Eton–Christ Church set, and send him at the age of fifteen to Hertford College, where Dr Newton had earlier established his reputation as an educational reformer. When his tutor wrote to him, 'Application like yours requires some intermission; and you are the only person with whom I have ever had connexion, to whom I could say this', it was no mere flattery; throughout his life Fox's correspondence attests the fact that, whatever his vagaries as a politician, gambler, and leader of Whig society, he remained what he had been at Oxford, a serious, passionate, and hard-working classical scholar. Dr Johnson's favourable view of Oxford (the most that he would admit was that some 'labefactation of principle' had set in) was coloured not only by his robust High Church Toryism, but by his friendship with Robert Chambers, Fellow and Tutor of University College. With Chambers, who succeeded Blackstone as Vinerian Professor of Law, and the two brothers Scott, who became the eminent judges Lord Stowell and Lord Eldon, University College enjoyed something of a renaissance in the second half of the eighteenth century.

WESLEY AT OXFORD

Lincoln, Christ Church and Pembroke Colleges had already produced the more surprising and explosive phenomenon of John and Charles Wesley and George Whitefield. John Wesley graduated at Christ Church in 1724, became a Fellow of Lincoln College in 1726, and in 1729 a tutor of the college. The 'Holy Club', which he organised between 1729 and his departure for Georgia in 1735, attracted, among others, his brother Charles from Christ Church, and George Whitefield, a servitor at Pembroke. Its influence at Oxford was never as wide as John Wesley had hoped. The Wesleyan movement only got under way when Whitefield initiated the practice of field-preaching. Wesley's last University sermon in 1744 reflected his disappointment:

73 Louis de Visme by Anton Raphael Mengs. Christ Church Hall

125

Are we, considered as a community of men, so filled with the Holy Ghost as to enjoy in our hearts, and show forth in our lives, the genuine fruits of that Spirit? Are all the Magistrates, all Heads and Governors of Colleges and Halls, and their respective Societies (not to speak of the inhabitants of the town) of one heart and Soul? Rather, have not pride and haughtiness of spirit, impatience and peevishness, sloth and indolence, gluttony and sensuality, and even a proverbial uselessness, been objected to us, perhaps not always by our enemies, not wholly without ground.

Blackstone commented, 'on mature deliberation it has been thought proper to punish him by a mortifying neglect'. The expulsion by the Vice-Chancellor of six Methodist undergraduates from St Edmund Hall in 1768 savoured of prejudice and persecution.

It is one of the tragic failures of Oxford and the Anglican Church in the eighteenth century that they failed to contain with the Church, as the Papacy in the thirteenth century had succeeded in containing the Franciscan movement, the religious genius of Wesley and White-field. Wesley himself remained what he had been at Oxford, an Arminian High Churchman, and in 1790 he wrote 'I live and die a member of the Church of England'. But by the time of his death, the movement had reached a point of no return. It was unfortunate that the religious 'enthusiasm' of the eighteenth century aroused inherited fears of the destructive 'fanaticism' of the seventeenth century. Bishop Butler told Wesley, 'Sir, the pretending to out-standing revelations and gifts of the Holy Ghost is a horrid thing, a very horrid thing'.

Even by the standard of the eighteenth century the spectacle of celibate clergymen who devoted themselves to gossiping, making bets, and drinking port in common-rooms, of professors who did not lecture, of undergraduates who were neither taught nor examined, was bizarre, and provided a rich field for the satirist. If the political involvement of the University goes far to explain its stagnation, it had also lost its function of leading the nation in intellectual adventure. Its main intellectual preoccupation was confined to combating deism and atheism by reconciling theology and the Newtonian cosmology. In this Bishop Butler was most successful in his *Analogy of Religion*.

SCIENCE IN THE EIGHTEENTH CENTURY

The prevailing theological and clerical atmosphere was not congenial to science: but even so the fading out of scientific research in Oxford after the remarkable flowering in the Common-wealth was surprisingly quick. John Mayow, Fellow of All Souls, wrote a treatise in 1668 on *Saltpetre and the Nitroaerian Spirit* which came near to the identification of oxygen, achieved by Lavoisier in the late eighteenth century. Mayow was a friend of Hooke, was elected a Fellow of the Royal Society in 1678, but died young in the following year. His work was not followed up.

In 1669 Robert Morison was elected the first Professor of Botany. Elias Ashmole, heir to his friend Tradescant's natural history collection, gave it in 1677 to the University on condition that a suitable building should be erected. The new Ashmolean Museum included a well-equipped chemical laboratory, but the University refused to endow a Chair of Chemistry. Instead Dr Robert Plot was appointed the first Keeper of the Museum in 1683, with the obligation to lecture in chemistry. He was for a short time Secretary of the Royal Society, and was a famous antiquarian and topographer, but his qualifications to lecture and research in chemistry are not obvious. He died in 1690: in 1710 the German savant Uffenbach found in his visit to Oxford that the laboratory equipment was unused and neglected. When Faraday demonstrated a spark produced by magnetic induction at a British Association meeting in

74 Provost's lodgings (1773–6). Worcester College

Oxford in 1837, an Oxford dignitary commented, 'Indeed, I am sorry for it; it is putting new arms into the hands of the incendiary.'

But it was not only in Oxford that the progress of science was halted. Despite the immense impetus to mathematical studies given by Newton, Cambridge produced little original work in the eighteenth century. By 1710 the Royal Society itself was in decline: Uffenbach reported that its laboratory was in a state of neglect as bad as in Oxford. Perhaps the Society had been too optimistic in promising immediate practical applications of science. Moreover it was being increasingly enervated by the invasion of aristocratic dilettantism.

Throughout Europe the first half of the eighteenth century cannot compare in creative originality with the seventeenth century, the 'century of genius'. It was a period of consolidation, classification, and diffusion of knowledge. Observational astronomy was steadily developed from the time of Newton by Flamsteed, the first Astronomer Royal, a Cambridge man; and then by Halley and Bradley, both Oxford men, and Savilian Professors. The Oxford Observatory was built by the Radcliffe trustees in the years following 1772.

In the second half of the eighteenth century the lead in scientific and medical studies was passing to the dissenting academies, to Birmingham and the Scottish universities of Edinburgh and Glasgow, and to France, where chemistry found its Newton in Lavoisier. Of the eighteenth century G. M. Trevelyan commented that 'the country houses, the Dissenting Academies, and the Scottish Universities did more than Oxford and Cambridge to nourish the widely diffused English culture of that period of our civilisation.'

6 The Era of Reform

The upas-tree of oligarchy was shaken by the American War of Independence. Failure in the war brought into question not only Lord North's government but the whole system of patronage. Middle class opinion brought organised pressure to bear in elections, and from the fall of North in 1782 government sinecures and patronage were steadily cut down. The Evangelical movement within the Church promoted new standards of responsibility and activity in public life.

This change in the political and intellectual climate was reflected even in the stagnant backwater of Oxford. The scandal of the obsolete university examinations was at last tackled by the combined influence of three powerful Heads of colleges, who had previously been active college tutors. Cyril Jackson became Dean of Christ Church in 1783, John Eveleigh Provost of Oriel in 1781, and John Parsons Master of Balliol in 1798. In 1800 they succeeded in passing the new Examination Statute. Instead of the Regent Masters, six public examiners were to be appointed by the University; in addition to the pass examination, there was to be an 'extraordinary examination' for candidates who wished to attempt it, in which the names should be placed in order of merit. Thus was established the basic principle of the Honours examination, though the statute was frequently remodelled between 1800 and 1830. In 1807 Mathematics was divided from Literae Humaniores, and separately classed. A First and Second Class replaced the list of names in order of merit. In 1809 a Third Class and in 1830 a Fourth Class were added. In 1808 Robert Peel established his reputation, and a record, as the first candidate to be awarded a Double First. If Honours candidates were at first few and exceptional, the new university examination set new standards all round, and college internal examinations began to be taken seriously.

An even more crucial breakthrough came through open competition for fellowships, and in this Oriel under Provost Eveleigh led the way, closely followed by Balliol.

By 1830 Oxford was perceptibly different from the Oxford of 1789. The Oxford Union Debating Society, where Gladstone was to make his reputation, started in 1825, and acquired its first premises in 1829. The first Oxford v. Cambridge cricket match was in 1827. Organised rowing was developing after 1825, and the first Oxford v. Cambridge boat race took place in 1829. Dr Jenkyns, the Master of Balliol, was induced to take a look at the new phenomenon of a racing eight and exclaimed with pleasure 'It is like the motion of one man!'. A minority of colleges were setting the example of higher academic standards. But the men who had made these changes were far from being radical; Eveleigh, Jackson and Parsons were staunch Anglican Tories. The basic structure of post-Restoration Oxford as the 'nursery of the Church'

76 Sir Thomas le Breton by Sir Thomas Lawrence (c. 1826) Pembroke College

remained untouched. The Revolutionary and Napoleonic wars had fortified the alliance of Church and King. Windham's slogan that 'it is impossible to repair one's house in a hurricane' prevailed over Fox's liberalism, and reform was frozen for the duration of the war. The horrors of the Revolution were imputed to irreligion, and Dissenters were accused of being crypto-Jacobins. Oxford enthusiastically voted the money to print a Bible for the use of the émigré French clergy. The high-water mark of anti-Jacobin Toryism in Oxford was the visit of the allied leaders in 1814, when the Prince Regent entertained the Tsar Alexander, the King of Prussia, and Marshal Blücher to an enormous banquet in the Radcliffe Camera.

By 1828 the Tory party which won the war was breaking up, and reform, so long delayed, threatened to be violent. The anomalies of the Church with which the University was so intimately connected were particularly glaring, and radical agitation was distinctly anti-clerical. In the Bristol Reform Bill riots in 1831, the Bishop's Palace was burnt down. In a riot at Oxford Dr Jenkyns, Master of Balliol, tried to intervene, with singular lack of success. He got no further than the words 'My deluded friends', when he received a paving-stone in the stomach, and retreated hastily behind the gates of Balliol.

NEWMAN AND ARNOLD

Yet the reform of the University was to be delayed for twenty years after the great Reform Act of 1832. The death-throes of the Anglican monopoly were to be prolonged and violent. Between 1828 and 1872 there was a continuous struggle for possession of the body and soul of Oxford. It was prolonged because the urge to reform Oxford developed sharply contradictory aims. It is ironic that from Oriel came both the protagonists in the struggle, John Henry Newman and Thomas Arnold. In 1815 Arnold was elected a Fellow of Oriel, and in 1822 Newman. When Newman arrived at Oriel, the College, with the exception of John Keble, was liberal and latitudinarian in theological thought. If the Fellows had been able to glimpse the future, they would have been startled to find that their new junior Fellow would end his career as a Cardinal of the Roman Church. While the 'orthodox two-bottle' High Churchmen of Oxford were content with a passive defence of vested interests, Arnold and Newman wished to revitalise the Church, but in sharply divergent ways. Arnold wanted a Church as comprehensive and national as possible, emphasising Christian morality and social justice rather than dogma. Newman was a man of powerful uncompromising intellect and spiritual force, a gifted writer and controversialist who had been brought up in the evangelical tradition. He viewed the issues of the day *sub specie aeternitatis*, and lifted the whole debate on to a high and rarefied plane. In his first years at Oriel he was under the influence of the latitudinarian Whately, but recoiled in horror from the consequences of liberalism in theology. It could only end in 'general scepticism'.

In 1828 concessions to dissent by the repeal of the Test and Corporation Acts, and in 1829 Catholic Emancipation, foreshadowed a general attack on the Anglican Establishment. At Oxford the cry was raised of 'the Church in danger', and Newman joined the campaign to oust Peel from the University seat in Parliament, for defaulting on the issue of Catholic Emancipation. It was at this point that Newman precipitated a quarrel in Oriel which tragically damaged the college. When Newman became a Tutor in 1826, the tutorial system as it emerged later in the century did not exist. The Tutors gave routine lectures to large classes, and Honours candidates who wanted individual tuition found their own private tutors, usually outside the college. Newman had many of the qualities of a great teacher, and his ideas foreshadowed the tutorial system as it was developed by Jowett of Balliol twenty years later. He wanted the Tutors to devote more time to individual tuition. By 1829 he had persuaded his colleagues to move in this direction. 'The bad men are thrown into large classes, and his time saved for the better sort, who are put into very small lectures, and principally with their own tutors quite familiarly and chattingly.' He now agreed with his colleagues on a plan which was presented to the Provost, Hawkins, as an 'ultimatum'. He wrote to the Provost, 'It is founded on these principles that the Tutors have full authority to arrange their lectures without consulting the Provost – an authority delegated to them by him in their being appointed Tutor and secondly that each Tutor is especially responsible for the instruction of the Pupils committed to him on entrance.' As Newman afterwards admitted, his handling of the proposal was tactless and uncompromising. By challenging the Provost's constitutional authority over the tutorial arrangements, he put Hawkins in an impossible position and ensured that the plan could not be considered on its merits: no Head of a college could submit to being excluded from the vital issue of the educational policy of the college. Hawkins had been supported by Newman in his election as Provost in 1828, in preference to Keble: but he was already suspicious of Newman's involvement in ecclesiastical politics, and sensed that he would be temperamentally incapable of drawing the line between pastoral care of a pupil and religious proselytising. He consulted his predecessor Copleston, now Bishop of Llandaff, who replied 'from what you say of Newman's religious views, I fear he is impracticable. His notion of dangers to Church and State I cannot understand.' Newman was backed to the hilt by his friends Wilberforce and Hurrell Froude, and the row ended in Hawkins' loss of the three ablest of his Tutors. Mark Pattison, who entered Oriel as an undergraduate in 1832, considered this affair to be 'the turning-point in the fortunes of Oriel. From this date the College began to go downhill, both in the calibre of the men who obtained Fellowships, and in the style and tone of the undergraduates. In the race for University Honours, Balliol rapidly shot ahead.'

Newman always looked back on Keble's University sermon in 1833 against 'national apostasy' as the beginning of the Oxford Movement, more precisely the Tractarian or Apostolic movement. The Tractarians maintained that the nation could only remain Christian if the Church reclaimed its Caroline and Laudian heritage as a branch of the Catholic and Apostolic Church, the true *via media* between schismatic Protestantism and the Roman Church perverted by the counter-reformation. 'It would be a second Reformation – a better Reformation for it would be a return not to the 16th century but to the 17th century'.

By this time the Whig government of Lord Grey had introduced an Irish Church Bill to suppress ten Irish Protestant bishoprics, and, under Radical pressure, was about to introduce bills for the abolition of university tests, and for the redistribution of the revenues of the Church in England. The Church appeared to be the helpless victim of unlimited State interference. If, as the Tractarians maintained, the Church was a divinely appointed institution by direct succession from the Apostles, such interference was sacrilege, regardless of the merits of the proposals. The Tractarians were therefore committed to the defence of the vested interests of the Church, and especially to Anglican control of the University as 'the nursery of the Church'.

Years later Pusey, the Tractarian Professor of Hebrew, was still contending that 'the problem and special work of an University is not how to advance science, not how to make discoveries ... but to form minds religiously, morally, intellectually'. 'All things must speak of God, refer to God, or they are atheistic. History, without God, is a chaos without design, an end, or aim. Political economy, without God, would be a selfish teaching about acquisition.

78 Formerly Canal House, now the Master's lodgings. St Peter College

79 Green Siberian marble vase given by Tsar Alexander I in 1816.
    Merton College Chapel
80 (opposite) Memorial to Percy Bysshe Shelley by Edward Onslow Ford
    (1893). University College

Physics, without God, would be but a dull enquiry into certain meaningless phenomena.' It was clear to the liberals, Arnold, and later to his pupil Stanley, to Benjamin Jowett and Mark Pattison that the Tractarians must be defeated before the University could be modernised.

The Tractarian movement quickly gained momentum. Newman launched the 'Tracts for the Times' which attracted especially the parochial clergy, whose massive votes as non-resident graduates of the University could control Convocation. The bishops were startled to be told that 'black event though it would be for the country, yet we could not wish them a more blessed termination of their course than the spoiling of their goods and martyrdom'. As Vicar of the University church of St Mary's since 1828, Newman used his pulpit to good effect to expound the principles of the movement. An Address to the Archbishop of Canterbury from the Laity of the Church of England, signed by the impressive number of 230,000 heads of families, extolled the Church's 'apostolic form of government'. The politicians were at least warned that the Church was still a force to be reckoned with.

A bill to abolish university tests passed the Commons but was defeated in the House of Lords by a large majority. A proposal to modify the tests promoted by the Hebdomadal Board in Oxford in 1835 was defeated in Convocation by a large majority of Tractarians and orthodox High Churchmen. The Duke of Wellington, leader of the ultra-Tories, had been enthusiastically elected as Chancellor of the University in succession to Lord Grenville in 1834. With his normal common sense the Duke pointed out to the Vice-Chancellor that the University should take care not to defend the indefensible. No change of government 'can render unnecessary an investigation by the authorities of the University into the state of their affairs, and the application of such temperate remedies as may be found necessary: because no changes can affect the existing composition of parliament and allay its inquisitorial jealousy of the institutions of the country'. An Ecclesiastical Commission, however, was inevitable, and Peel did not hesitate to appoint it, in his brief ministry of 1834.

When in 1836 Melbourne appointed as Regius Professor of Divinity a liberal theologian, Hampden, who had advocated the admission of Dissenters to the University, the Tractarians signified their displeasure by forcing a statute through Convocation depriving him of a vote in the election of Select Preachers to the University. Arnold publicly denounced the Tractarians as 'the Oxford Malignants'.

Almost as rapidly as it had spread the Tractarian movement broke up on the rocks of its own internal contradictions. Its leader Newman was losing faith in his own cause. As early as 1839, his study of the early Church Councils had raised doubts in his minds about the *via media*. 'The thought for the moment had been "The Church of Rome will be found right after all":
and then it had vanished.' Early in 1841 he published Tract No. 90, which brought to a head the gathering suspicion as to the popery of the Tractarians. Newman attempted to demonstrate that the Thirty-Nine Articles of the Anglican Church allowed for a catholic interpretation. The Tract was condemned by the university authorities, and by numerous bishops. Newman submitted to the Bishop of Oxford's ruling that the Tracts must be discontinued: but he wrote in a letter at this time 'what is the inevitable and immediate effect of the Church of England by its rulers declaring that she is not that Holy Catholic Church but to send people to Rome by exhaustion because there is no other Church?'

Further blows followed. The Martyrs' Memorial to Cranmer, Latimer and Ridley was built by subscription in 1839 as a Protestant counterblast to the Tractarians. A Lutheran was appointed to the Bishopric of Jerusalem with the approval of the Anglican hierarchy. In 1843 a University sermon by Pusey was condemned by the Hebdomadal Board, and he was

81   St Ignatius Loyola, attributed to Juan Martinez Montañes (1568–
1649). Campion Hall

suspended from preaching for three years. In this year Newman resigned as Vicar of St Mary's and went into retreat at Littlemore. In 1845 a book on the *Ideal of a Christian Church* by W.G. Ward, an extreme Tractarian Fellow of Balliol, was condemned by Convocation, and Ward was deprived of his degrees. A censure of Tract 90 by Convocation was averted only by the veto of the Proctors. At the end of 1845 Newman was received into the Roman Church. 'The men who had driven me from Oxford were distinctly the liberals.' 'I found no fault with the liberals: they had beaten me in a fair field.'

LIBERAL REFORM

The victory of the liberals over the Tractarians in Oxford opened the way for university reform. Mark Pattison, Fellow and later Rector of Lincoln, who under the spell of Newman was 'drawn into the whirlpool of Tractarianism' and hesitated on the verge of following Newman into the Roman Church in 1845, wrote bitterly in his later Memoirs of a 'nightmare which had oppressed Oxford for fifteen years. For so long we had been given over to discussions unprofitable in themselves and which had entirely diverted our thoughts from the business of the place.'

The second Whig government of Lord Melbourne (1835–41) was too weak to press the case for a government commission on the universities, and during the Conservative government of 1841–6, Wellington and Peel took the line that the universities were reforming themselves. But there were few signs of progress in this direction: in 1839 proposals to strengthen the professoriate were defeated by Convocation.

The return of a Whig government in 1846 revived the issue; and by this time the academic liberals in Oxford despaired of the University's reforming itself, and welcomed a government commission. Arnold's premature death in 1842 was balanced by the arrival on the scene of the young Benjamin Jowett, closely connected with Arnold's pupils, Stanley and Tait. When Tait succeeded Arnold as Headmaster of Rugby, Jowett took Tait's place as a Tutor of Balliol at the age of 25. He supported a parliamentary motion in 1844 for a commission of inquiry, and in 1847 he explained the standpoint of the academic liberals in a letter to Roundell Palmer, later to be Lord Chancellor. 'Let me ask what chance there is of reform from within ... It is nobody's fault, we cannot reform ourselves ... On the other hand, is it at all probable that we shall be allowed to remain as we are for twenty years longer; the one solitary exclusive, unnational Corporation, our enormous wealth without any manifest utilitarian purpose; a place, the studies of which belong to the past, and unfortunately seem to have no power of incorporating new branches of knowledge.' In 1850 the Prime Minister, Lord John Russell, suddenly adopted the motion of a radical backbencher, and announced the setting up of a Royal Commission to enquire into the universities of Oxford and Cambridge. As all the Oxford Commissioners were without exception Oxford academic liberals, including Tait, and Stanley as Secretary, the battle with the conservative, clerical opposition was fairly joined.

The Vice-Chancellor contested the legality of the Commission and vainly petitioned the Queen to cancel it. The Bishop of Exeter, Visitor of Exeter College, described it as an inquisition which had 'absolutely no parallel since the fatal attempt of King James II to subject the colleges to his unhallowed control'. Only seven of the nineteen colleges were prepared to co-operate with the Commission. Owing to this passive resistance the Commissioners were unable to elucidate college finances, but they received massive evidence from individuals. When they reported in 1852 in restrained but trenchant terms, Gladstone, hitherto hostile to

82   Keble College Chapel (1868–82) by William Butterfield

83 Venetian windows (1890) by Sir Thomas Graham Jackson,
seen from a window on the hall staircase. Hertford College

government interference, was converted. He was now Chancellor of the Exchequer in the Aberdeen government, and threw himself whole-heartedly into passing an Oxford University Act which would give effect to the Report. He warned his Oxford constituents that if his Bill failed to pass 'no other half so favourable would ever again be brought in'. The Act of 1854 appointed Executive Commissioners with statutory powers to frame statutes for the University and colleges, unless they had satisfactorily recast their own statutes by a given date.

The Commission of Inquiry had directed attention to the main needs for reform – the government of the University, the 'narrow oligarchy' of the Heads of Houses and the legislature of Convocation dominated by non-resident clerics, the narrowness of the curriculum and the neglect of scientific, medical and legal studies, the barriers to recruitment by merit raised by the numerous fellowships and scholarships tied to founders' kin and localities, the extravagant cost of education encouraged by the obsolete distinction of rank afforded to noblemen and gentlemen-commoners. The Commissioners were impressed by the evidence of Frederick Temple of Balliol that the 'Fellows have become the head of the University and cannot now be dislodged. The nation is bound to see that they are the ablest men which the University can supply.'

The sanctions wielded by the Executive Commission ensured that by the end of the decade reforms along these lines, though not always in the precise form recommended by the Commission of Inquiry, were implemented. The new Hebdomadal Council contained professors and elected members of Congregation as well as the Vice-Chancellor, Proctors and six Heads of Houses. A new Congregation of resident members considered all legislation. Convocation retained its right to accept or reject, but could no longer amend. Professorial salaries were raised and subsidised from the suppression of sinecure college fellowships. College statutes were remodelled to throw open fellowships and scholarships. The Vice-Chancellor was empowered to license Private Halls for poorer students.

Gladstone had launched his Bill with the intention of preserving the Anglican monopoly of the University, but he was forced to agree to an amendment abolishing religious tests for undergraduates and Bachelors. The government of the University and the colleges remained confined to members of the Church of England, and the majority of Fellows remained celibate clergymen. The clerical monopoly had been shaken but it remained for the time being dominant. Writing about the Prince of Wales to her eldest daughter, the Crown Princess of Prussia, in 1859, Queen Victoria could say, 'Today dear Papa has gone to Oxford to see how Bertie is getting on in that old monkish place which I have a horror of'. In retrospect, however, the Commissions of the 1850s appear as the turning-point in the evolution of the University in the nineteenth century. Like the Parliamentary Reform Act of 1832, it was a halfway house which opened the way to further reform. Its effectiveness lay in the co-operation between Parliament and the academic reformers; by relieving their frustrations, it gave them their chance. Mark Pattison wrote in his Memoirs, 'If any Oxford man had gone to sleep in 1846 and woken up again in 1850 he would have found himself in a totally different world'.

By 1871 Pusey had to lament that 'Oxford was lost to the Church of England'. After continual agitation for a decade Gladstone himself took charge of a University Tests Bill, which became law in 1871. Religious tests were abolished except for theological degrees and professorships. In the same year Gladstone announced that he would set up an inquiry into the University and college revenues and endowments. The reaction in the University was markedly different from that of 1850, and the Vice-Chancellor had assured Gladstone of the University's co-operation. The reforms launched by the 1851 Commission, the rising tide of matriculations from 1862 onwards, the broadening of studies, had created a new situation in the University which required parliamentary legislation to free more college endowments for university use. In 1877 it was a Conservative government that gave effect to the changes based on the Royal Commission appointed by Gladstone in 1872.

The 1872 Commission found that the endowment income of the University was £47,000, while the combined income of the colleges and Halls amounted to £367,000. It was inevitable that the colleges should be asked to make a greater contribution to university needs. A Common University Fund was established, to which colleges were required to contribute according to their means. The wealthier colleges were required to support many more university professorships and readerships. Professors and Readers were required to lecture regularly and four Boards of Faculties, of Theology, Law, Arts and Sciences, were to publish lists of lectures. Fellowships were no longer to be held for life, and prize fellowships were limited to seven years. Conditions of celibacy or ordination were no longer to be attached to fellowships. The Private Halls envisaged by the 1851 Commission had proved to be a failure, too often becoming a refuge for the idle or incompetent. Most of the remaining ancient Halls were now sentenced to absorption in the colleges. The financial forecasts of the 1872 Commission proved to be too optimistic: they could not have foreseen the onset of the prolonged agricultural depression after 1879, 'the black year of British agriculture', which severely reduced the income of the colleges. The clerical party found some compensation for the loss of control of the University in the foundation in 1870 of Keble College, launched by public subscription as a memorial to John Keble, who died in 1866.

At about the same time Thomas Baring, a member of the great banking family, offered a benefaction to endow a college and scholarships. Magdalen Hall, which had proved itself to be the most vigorous of the Halls in the nineteenth century, with an undergraduate population higher than many of the colleges, received the benefaction after it had been declined by Brasenose College, and became the new Hertford College by Act of Parliament in 1874.

THE AGE OF JOWETT

The period 1850–90 in Oxford may not unfairly be called the Age of Jowett. It is an age embarrassingly rich in remarkable personalities, to mention only a few – Dean Liddell of Christ Church, Stanley, later Dean of Westminster, Mark Pattison, Matthew Arnold, Ruskin, William Morris, C. L. Dodgson (Lewis Carroll), Acland – and in a complicated academic democracy such as Oxford no one man dominates the scene. But the theme of this essay is the evolution of the University, and it cannot be denied that in shaping the character of the University as it emerged at the end of the century Jowett's was the greatest single influence. It is still not easy to analyse exactly how or why this puny clergyman, handicapped by shyness all his life, made such an impact on Balliol College, the University, and the political world. His rule as Master of Balliol was marked by a steadily rising tide of success for the college, but not by dramatic changes. He was a highly competent and effective Vice-Chancellor from 1882 to 1886, but by then the main Victorian reforms had been effected. The legend that Jowett created the eminence of Balliol has been dissipated. The foundations of Balliol's success had been firmly laid, before Jowett became a Fellow of Balliol, under two successive Masters, Parsons and Jenkyns. It was said of Jenkyns that, though he was an old-fashioned High Church Tory, he had an 'infallible eye for a clever man, as a jockey has of a horse' and he was wise enough to back his young Tutors, even when he instinctively disapproved of their policy. By 1830 Balliol had drawn level with Oriel in attracting candidates for fellowships by open competition. The academic prestige of Oriel took a long time to recover from its involvement in the Tractarian movement, and the lead passed indisputably to Balliol.

What, then, was Jowett's precise contribution? As a leader of the academic liberals, even as a young Fellow in the 1840s, he had great influence on the thinking of the 1851 and 1872 Commissions. That he possessed an intuitive and a quick perception of the essential and the practicable, combined with great force of character and will, seldom selfishly directed, which would have made him a great civil servant and administrator, is clear from his letters and his evidence to the Commissions. It was said of Jowett as Vice-Chancellor 'You can just occasionally beat Jowett, but you have to stay up all night to do it'.

But his real achievement belongs to the long period of his tutorship at Balliol, before he became Master. It consisted in realising, so fully that it became a pattern for the whole university, the potentialities of the tutorial system implicit in the peculiar evolution of Oxford as a collegiate university. The qualities and methods of a great teacher are difficult to analyse, as they are so personal. In one of his best satires Stephen Leacock described the tutorial process as 'being smoked at by one's tutor'. Jowett himself seldom defined his methods. In an obituary of one of his most brilliant pupils, who died young as a Tutor of Christ Church, he wrote, 'He understood perfectly the secret of success as a College Tutor. The secret is chiefly devotion to the work, and consideration for the characters of young men.' One of Jowett's pupils, Brodrick, later Warden of Merton, came nearest to the secret: 'His greatest skill consisted, like that of Socrates, in helping us to learn and think for ourselves.' In later life, Jowett disapproved of T. H. Green imposing on his pupils a particular system of metaphysics. His concept of the process of higher education is now such a commonplace truism that the originality and extent of Jowett's example has been lost to sight. For it is clear from Newman's experience at Oriel that in the clerical Oxford of the first half of the nineteenth century, when Jowett first became a Tutor, the tutorial function was very imperfectly grasped. Jowett once said that he 'wished to inoculate the world with Balliol'. In this respect he succeeded. Consciously or not, all university teachers throughout the English-speaking world are influenced by the example of Jowett.

Jowett's openness of mind which helped him to become a great teacher exposed him, in the middle of his career, to controversy and even persecution. Doubts about his religious views may have cost him the Mastership of Balliol in 1854, when Jenkyns died. He was a contributor to the volume of *Essays and Reviews* in 1860, which raised one of the greatest theological storms of the century. The passions aroused by this book can be explained only against the background of the impact of Darwinism on the Victorian mind. In the same year, at a famous meeting of the British Association at the Science Museum in Oxford, Huxley had worsted Samuel Wilberforce, Bishop of Oxford, in a debate on Darwin's *Origin of Species*. The intellectual panic caused by Darwin was as great, or greater, than that caused by Galileo in the seventeenth century, and the Churchmen who wrote *Essays and Reviews* were reviled for selling the pass of faith and dogma to scientific rationalism.

Yet Jowett's essay 'On the Interpretation of Scripture' said no more than this: 'It is to be interpreted, like other books, with attention to the character of its author, and the prevailing state of civilisation and knowledge, with allowance for peculiarities of style and language, and words of thought and figures of speech. Yet not without a sense that as we read there grows upon us the witness of God in the world.'

Pusey, with some Evangelical support, trundled out the rusty engine of the Vice-Chancellor's court against Jowett, citing him for 'infringing the Statutes and privileges of the University by promulgating 'certain erroneous and strange doctrines contrary to and inconsistent with the doctrines of the Church of England'. The prosecution collapsed when the legal assessor to the court refused to exercise jurisdiction. Jowett's private comment on the affair was that, 'In a few years there will be no religion among intellectual young men, unless religion is shown to be consistent with criticism.' It was also on theological grounds that the Cathedral Chapter of Christ Church for years refused to supplement Jowett's nominal stipend of £40 a year as Regius Professor of Greek.

One important effect of these theological controversies was to ensure that Jowett remained in Oxford, by eliminating the risk that he would be removed by ecclesiastical preferment. In 1865 he wrote to Florence Nightingale, the woman he came nearest to marrying, 'I am not going to give up the young life of Oxford (so full of hope) for the dead man's bones of a Cathedral town'. It may seem disproportionate to give so much attention to one remarkable man, but Jowett was both the catalyst and the symbol of the University as it emerged, secularised and reformed, by the end of the century.

The system for which Jowett stood was effective, by and large, in educating the rulers of a great Empire. But at the height of his success Jowett aroused criticism on several counts. He was accused of being a 'tuft-hunter', cultivating only the important and the successful. This charge was misconceived. Jowett once admitted that 'he had a great prejudice against all persons who do not succeed in the world'. By this he did not mean material success; he felt it was wicked that men should not use their talents to the full in whatever direction they lay. He took endless pains to save the poet Swinburne from disaster. From 1850 onwards he was constantly promoting ways and means of bringing poor students to the University. As early as 1852 he drew up a scheme for a Hall annexed to Balliol, where students could go through university at a cost of £50 a year. In 1866 he persuaded the college to put this into effect, and Balliol Hall was started in charge of the philosopher T.H.Green. Jowett wrote, 'At present not a tenth or twentieth part of the ability of the country comes to the University'. In 1867 he wrote to Earl Russell that 'it is very important to provide a means of giving the best education to the best intelligence in every class of Society'. He supported the repeal in 1868 of the statute requiring residence in a college or Hall. In advance of his generation Jowett foresaw the time when the University would be open to ability from every class. He was also a pioneer in campaigning for the extension of university education in the great cities.

The second count against Jowett was that he exalted the college tutorial system at the expense of research. Mark Pattison wrote that 'the separation between Jowett and myself is a difference upon the fundamental question of University politics viz. Science and learning v. School Keeping'. Certainly Jowett always put first the liberal education of young men. He was even attacked for giving official recognition as Vice-Chancellor to amateur dramatic perform-ances by undergraduates which in course of time were to provide many notable actors for the English stage. He was suspicious of Mark Pattison's advocacy of the indiscriminate endowment of research, divorced from teaching. He supported the development of inter-collegiate lectures, and maintained that college and professorial teaching were complementary. As Professor of Greek he had set an example of conscientious lecturing. But it was only towards the end of his life that he appreciated the immense resources, human and material, which were to be involved in keeping pace with scientific research, and regretted his ignorance of natural science. In 1891 he said to Acland, 'the great thing now is attention to Physical Science'.

84 *An Elderly Woman with Clasped Hands* by Mathis Nithart, called Grünewald (*c.* 1478–1528). Ashmolean Museum

This was a problem which could no longer be evaded by the University, and increasingly as it advanced into the twentieth century. The thin trickle of Oxford science in the eighteenth century began to flow more strongly in the nineteenth century, although it was held back by the theological preoccupations of the first half of the century. While English science was resuming its advance after 1760, science in Oxford lagged far behind until 1850. There had been signs of some revival in the period 1760–90, when Thomas Beddoes, a brilliant scientist and lecturer, who was in correspondence with Lavoisier, was appointed Dr Lee's Reader at Christ Church in 1788, and drew large audiences. But his sympathy with French Jacobinism drove him from the University in 1793.

Paradoxically the reform of the Examination Statute in 1800 worsened the position of science. There was no provision in the Honours examination for natural science beyond physics, which meant no more than elementary applied mathematics. On paper the University had a substantial and expanding corps of university teachers of science. Aldrich endowed two professorships in medicine and one in chemistry in 1803. The Prince Regent endowed readerships in mineralogy and geology. By 1820 there were altogether five professorships and seven readerships. But the salaries were so low that the posts were usually held in plurality, and laboratory space was confined to the Old Ashmolean, the Anatomy School built in Christ Church in 1767, and a few attics of the Clarendon Building. The professors complained that the classical bias of the new curriculum caused a steady dwindling of their lecture audiences. They met with little sympathy from the clerical majority in Oxford, for whom scientific studies were irrelevant, and possibly dangerous, to the purpose of the University. Buckland, who had been an eminent Reader in Geology before he became Dean of Westminster, wrote in 1847 that 'the idle part of the young men will do nothing and the studious portion will throw their attention into the channel of honours and profits which can alone be gained by the staple subjects of examinations for Degrees and Fellowships'. In his Memoirs Mark Pattison wrote 'Science was placed under a ban by the theologians who instinctively felt that it was fatal to their speculations.' One enraged supporter of the professoriate pointed out that 'Professors were not even prayed for in University Sermons'.

The leaders in the battle for science in Oxford in the first half of the nineteenth century – Buckland, Baden-Powell, Daubeny – were, if not brilliant original scientists, enthusiastic, active and public-spirited. Daubeny, Professor of Chemistry since 1822, refitted the Old Ashmolean Laboratory and built at his own expense a laboratory in the Botanic Gardens. In 1848, Henry Acland, appointed Lee's Reader in Anatomy, joined the ranks of the reformers. Their efforts would still have been in vain but for the increasing threat of government interference by a Royal Commission. At first the reformers were inclined to press the line that attendance at science lectures and some knowledge of science for the first degree should be made compulsory. It was probably no misfortune that a statute to this effect was defeated in 1839, as it became increasingly clear that science could gain a footing in the University only by establishing its own Honours examinations.

The crucial stages in the battle were won in 1850 when a new Examination Statute created a Final Honour School of Natural Science (as well as one of Law and Modern History), and in 1854 when the plan of the new University Science Museum was finally passed. But until a further statute was passed in 1864, which allowed a single Honours examination to qualify for a degree, Honours candidates had to take Literae Humaniores, and one or other of the new

Honours Examinations. It was not till 1886 that classics ceased to be a compulsory part of the intermediate examination, Moderations.

THE UNIVERSITY MUSEUM OF SCIENCE

The project for a new Museum of Science was mooted in 1847, but a proposal to use for this purpose a large part of the accumulated £60,000 profit of the University Press was defeated in Convocation. It was ridiculed as a 'receptacle for dried insects', a 'gigantic Babylon'; the profits of the Press were 'derived from a very sacred source, the profits upon the privilege of printing God's Word'. It required the support of the 1851 Commissioners, and the powerful advocacy of Acland to gain the day in 1853. Acland's unquestioned piety, his friendship with Pusey, as well as with Liddell and Jowett and Ruskin, his eminence as a scientist and as a practising physician, made him the ideal mediator between the factions. He persuaded Pusey and the Tractarians to vote for the scheme, and enlisted Ruskin's support in the choice of Woodward's design for the Museum, described as 'Rhenish Gothic'. Ruskin wrote, 'No other architecture, as I felt in an instant, could have thus adapted itself to a new and strange office.' What better design could there be for a chemical laboratory than a replica of the Abbot's kitchen at Glastonbury, discharging through its medieval chimneys the noxious fumes of its furnaces? Surrounded by the austere temples of twentieth-century science, the Museum remains a characteristic and moving symbol of the uneasy mid-Victorian reconciliation of science and religion. The Victorians would have spared themselves much agony of mind, much heat and friction, if they had listened more carefully to Acland's wise advice that they should not allow themselves to be agitated by the possible theological implications of a particular scientific theory, as these theories were constantly subject to revision. In his Will, Acland wrote, 'I pray that the faithful study of all nature may in Oxford and elsewhere lead men to the knowledge and love of God.'

Curious as its architecture was (Abbot's kitchen and all) the Museum gave to science by 1860 a centre of its own, capable of expansion. Its value was enhanced by the removal of the Radcliffe science library from the Camera to the Museum; in due course, in 1901, the Drapers' Company of London endowed the building of a new science library.

Oxford was now in a position to attract and to produce scientists of the first rank. The first in a new line of distinguished professors, and the first to occupy the Museum, was Benjamin Brodie, who succeeded Daubeny as Professor of Chemistry in 1855. With the appointment of Burdon Sanderson as the first Professor of Physiology in 1883, medical studies acquired a firm scientific basis, despite obstruction from the anti-vivisectionists, who condemned the new Physiology Laboratory as 'a chamber of horrors'. The great physiologist Sherrington was appointed to the chair in 1913. But for many years the college science laboratories continued to be an important supplement to the Museum. In 1877 Trinity combined with Balliol to expand the chemical laboratory started in a Balliol cellar in 1851. In 1854, Vernon Harcourt, pupil of Brodie and of the great Balliol mathematical tutor Henry Smith, was appointed Lee's Reader at Christ Church, where he carried on important research in the Anatomy School adapted as a chemical laboratory. Through his pupils he gave a powerful impetus to the development of Oxford chemistry. In 1905 the college laboratories increased their effectiveness by an agreement to specialise. Inorganic chemistry was concentrated in Christ Church, and physical chemistry in Balliol and Trinity and the Daubeny Laboratory at Magdalen, with the addition of a new laboratory in Jesus College from 1908. From 1919 an organic chemistry

86   Tympanum over the entrance to 62, Banbury Road (1864)
87   *(overleaf)* Chinoiserie bridge over the River Cherwell from St Hilda's College

laboratory at Queen's College supplemented the work of the Museum. The rapid growth of the science area round the Museum to house the expanding scientific departments belongs to the history of the twentieth century; the last college laboratory did not close till 1948.

NEW HONOUR SCHOOLS

The 'liberation of studies' by the institution of new Honour Schools, though it was won at the cost of increasing specialisation, brought new life to the curriculum, and not only in natural science. Literae Humaniores developed into a Final School of Philosophy and Ancient History: Modern History and Law, separated in 1872, steadily progressed in numbers and quality.

The study of modern languages raised the same problem as was the case for natural science, that of finding a place in an Honours examination. As far back as 1724 the Whig government of George I had tried to promote the study of European languages in the University, to provide qualified recruits for diplomacy, by founding a Regius Chair of Modern History backed by language teachers and King's scholarships. But the scheme languished as the government could provide only a handful of posts for the King's scholars, in face of the control of the diplomatic service by aristocratic patronage. In 1788 Sir Robert Taylor, a fashionable sculptor and architect, left in his will a benefaction of £60,000 for 'teaching and improving the European languages'. When the University finally received the benefaction in 1835, it was decided to build a Taylorian Institution at the corner of Beaumont Street, combined with an art gallery, the New Ashmolean Museum. Charles Cockerell won the competition for the design 'required to be of a Grecian character'. Completed in 1844, in the tide of the Gothic Revival, its merits were hardly appreciated at the time, and have now been revealed by cleaning. The development of a Taylorian Library was an important supplement to the Bodleian, but by 1877 the average size of classes in modern languages was only forty. In 1887 a proposal to create a new Honour School of Modern Languages, including English, was narrowly defeated. But in 1894 an Honour School of English Language and Literature was created, and in 1903 one of Modern Languages.

THE WOMEN'S COLLEGES

One epoch-making development of the Victorian age, the higher education of women, was beyond Jowett's range of vision, despite his wide circle of women friends. London and Cambridge led the way in this development, with the foundation of Bedford College, London, in 1849, and, at Cambridge, of Newnham in 1869 and Girton in 1873. In 1870 Oxford University gave permission to its Delegacy of Local Examinations to examine girls in secondary education. They were immediately faced with a portent of the future. To their embarrassment, Balliol and Worcester Colleges, which offered exhibitions to the successful candidates in the Oxford Local Examinations, found that the candidate at the top of the list in 1873 was a girl, Annie Rogers. She subsequently became one of the first women tutors in Oxford, and a leader in the campaign for the higher education of women at Oxford. In 1875 the Delegacy of Local Examinations was empowered to organise examinations of Honours standard for women.

By this time the celibate atmosphere of Oxford was changing, with the appearance of married Fellows of Colleges, some of whom co-operated in organising lectures for women. In 1878

Lady Margaret Hall (named after the Lady Margaret Beaufort, mother of King Henry VII) and in 1879 Somerville College (named after Mary Somerville, the scientist and astronomer), started as hostels for a handful of women students, followed by St Hugh's in 1886, and St Hilda's in 1893. At the same time an Association for the Higher Education of Women was formed to organise tuition for these students and the more numerous students who lived at home. The Oxford home-students were ultimately to develop into St Anne's College. In 1882 Somerville led the way in the appointment of a resident woman tutor for their own students.

In 1884 the Delegacy of Local Examinations was allowed to use certain of the university Honours examinations for examining women students instead of devising their own. This measure was not unopposed: Dean Burgon preached a hilarious sermon in New College Chapel in which he reminded the women that 'inferior to us God made you, and inferior to the end of time you will remain. But you are none the worse off for that.' Pusey thought the appearance of women's Halls 'one of the greatest misfortunes that has happened to us even in our own time in Oxford'. By 1894 all degree examinations were open to women, and most university and inter-collegiate lectures. The custom of requiring chaperones for women at lectures was quietly dropped.

Yet with a logic worthy of the university which produced Lewis Carroll, the University did not officially recognise the presence or existence of women students as members of the University. In 1896 Congregation rejected a resolution to confer the B.A. degree on women. Some of the opposition, including Lewis Carroll (C.L.Dodgson) hoped that the question would be evaded by the development of a separate women's university: but the trend had already become irreversible. One commentator on the 1896 debates wrote, 'The novelty of the proposal will wear off, and the fears, at once perfectly natural and perfectly unreasonable, which drove many members of the University to the verge of panic will die away.'

In 1907 ten women students obtained First Class Honours. When Lord Curzon became Chancellor of the University in 1907, he pointed out the anomalies of the situation, but being a staunch political opponent of female suffrage, he was obliged to find reasons for distinguishing between degrees and votes for women.

In 1910 the proposal for a 'Delegacy for the supervision of women students' passed through Congregation with surprising ease. A Principal of Home Students was officially recognised, as well as of the four residential 'Societies'. At the outbreak of the 1914–18 war, a Committee of Council initiated by the Senior Proctor was redrafting a statute for the admission of women to degrees. The social transformations of the war and the granting of women's suffrage in 1918 swept away further opposition. In 1920 a statute admitting women to full membership of the University was not contested.

89 Bas-relief from the palace of King Ashur-nasir-pal (883–859 BC).
Magdalen College

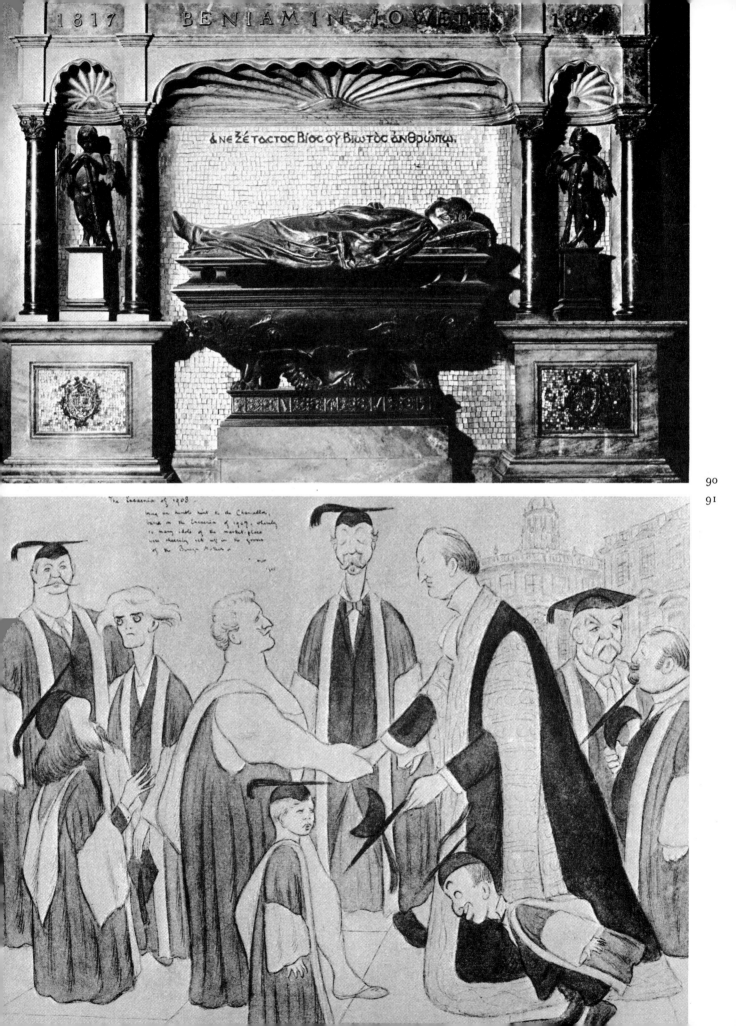

7 Oxford in the Twentieth Century

The forces which were to shape the University in the twentieth century were already perceptible at the end of the nineteenth – the higher education of women, the expansion of science, the opening of the University to wider sectors of the community. Change was greatly accelerated by the effects of two world wars. By the end of the first world war, as has been seen, women had won their place in the University.

In the second half of the nineteenth century the complacency which prevailed at the time of the Great Exhibition of 1851 about Britain's lead in science and technology had been undermined. Increasingly Britain was seen to be lagging behind an industrialised Germany with its new science-based industries supported by a large corps of professional scientists. A major, if belated, step was taken with the passing of the Balfour Education Act of 1902, which ensured a large expansion of State secondary education. By creating a demand for science graduates as secondary school teachers, it also promoted a rapid expansion of scientific education in the universities – a demand which industry had mostly been too slow and too short-sighted to create for itself.

In the first world war the aeroplane, the tank and radio played a significant part, and emphasised the national importance of scientific research and education. And Oxford's contribution to the war effort was not merely in scientific research. Not only do the appalling statistics of the college war memorials record the sacrifice of its senior and junior members, but dons demonstrated their versatility in applying science to warfare, in the intelligence services, and in administration.

It was largely, however, the needs of scientific research that led to the first government grant of £100,000 a year to Oxford and to Cambridge in 1922. Chemistry was now outgrowing the college laboratories, and in 1916 organic chemistry was equipped with a new building, through the benefaction of C. W. Dyson Perrins. Here, first Perkin and then Robinson developed flourishing schools of research. After the war Dr Lee's Professorship in Chemistry was created from an earlier foundation to take care of Physical and Inorganic Chemistry. The first holder of the new Chair was Professor F. Soddy, who in 1921 became the first Oxford professor to win a Nobel Prize. It was not till 1941 that, under his successor C. N. Hinshelwood, a large new physical chemistry building arose, financed by a benefaction from Lord Nuffield.

In 1919 F. A. Lindemann (later Lord Cherwell) was appointed to Dr Lee's Chair of Experimental Philosophy. His predecessor Clifton, appointed as far back as 1865, had designed and built the first Clarendon Laboratory in 1872. Its name records one of the more

90 Memorial to Benjamin Jowett by Edward Onslow Ford (1894).
    Balliol College Chapel
91 Max Beerbohm, *The Encaenia of 1908*. Ashmolean Museum

curious episodes of Oxford finance. The grandson of the Earl of Clarendon had directed in 1751 that the proceeds of the sale of publication of the Earl's papers should be devoted to the building of a riding-school in Oxford. It was not till 1860 that sufficient funds accumulated, and the trustees were then persuaded to build a laboratory instead. Thereafter the laboratory remained as it was built in 1872: in 1919 it did not even have mains electricity.

Lindemann did not fulfil his early promise in original research but he fostered modern physics in Oxford, and by the time of his retirement in 1956 he had put the Clarendon Laboratory in the same class as the Cavendish at Cambridge, overtaking the long lead established by Clerk-Maxwell, Thomson and Rutherford. He took an active part in helping scientists escaping from Nazi persecution, and found support for several of them in his laboratory from 1933 onwards. Probably the best deed he did for Oxford science was to bring there from Breslau Franz (later Sir Francis) Simon, the low-temperature physicist, who succeeded him as Professor in 1956, though he died shortly after. By 1939 thirty candidates were taking Physics Finals, and many of his pupils were to play important parts in the second world war. He had built a new Clarendon Laboratory by 1940.

TIZARD AND LINDEMANN

In view of the pre-eminence of the Cavendish at Cambridge, it is surprising that the most influential scientific statesmen of Britain in the second world war, Tizard and Lindemann, came from Oxford. Both were drawn into aeronautical research and testing in the first world war, and both made a special contribution to the winning of the second world war, and indirectly to the development of scientific education. It was Tizard who ensured that radar should become fully operational in time for the Battle of Britain in 1940, by winning the confidence of the RAF and mobilising the university scientists. Lindemann's contribution came in a different way: by winning the confidence and friendship of Winston Churchill he ensured that the Prime Minister and Minister of Defence should be constantly and daily aware of the importance of the application of science to the war. In the perspective of history these achievements far outweigh the effects of the quarrel between these two powerful men, which has all the inevitability of Greek tragedy, and has been given melodramatic treatment by C. P. Snow. The famous quarrel was summed up in one lapidary phrase when R. V. Jones, head of Air Ministry scientific intelligence, and Lindemann's former pupil (now Professor of Natural Philosophy at the University of Aberdeen) went to discuss with him in 1942 the use of 'Window', the dropping of tinfoil strips to confuse the German radar defence. Lindemann remarked, 'You will find both Tizard and myself united against you.' To which R. V. Jones retorted 'Well, if I have achieved that, by God, I have achieved something.'

The decisive part played by radar in the Battle of Britain, closely followed by the development of the atomic bomb, was a turning-point not only in the war but in the development of higher education in Britain. The lesson of the first world war had been only half-learned and had been largely forgotten between the wars. Few outside the universities had grasped the startling implications of the work of Rutherford in nuclear physics, of Keynes in economics, of Florey on penicillin.

After 1940 there could be no doubt about the importance of investment in higher education. Lord Hankey, who had started his career as a protégé of Fisher, the moderniser of the Navy, and had been one of the progenitors of the tank, was in charge of war-time and preparatory post-war planning of higher education. The Butler Act of 1944 accepted the financial responsibility of the State to ensure that ability was not lost to the universities. By the end of the first post-war decade the university population in Britain had doubled: by the end of the second decade it was accepted that this figure should be more than doubled again. Oxford and Cambridge were now part of a constellation of expanding universities. Science at Oxford has long since exchanged the role of Cinderella for that of *prima donna:* with forty-one Fellows of the Royal Society, including three Nobel prize-winners, in its expanding and proliferating departments. Of a total of some 7,000 undergraduate students, nearly 2,500 are now reading scientific subjects.

It has been necessary to dwell on some of the main developments of science in Oxford in the twentieth century, because it is still widely assumed that Oxford is predominantly an arts university. The great Faculties of Literae Humaniores and Modern History, for example, are indeed still the largest in the country: but in contrast with the nineteenth century, the careers of arts graduates are no longer confined to the Church, teaching, politics and government service, and the learned professions. In the last thirty years industry and commerce have

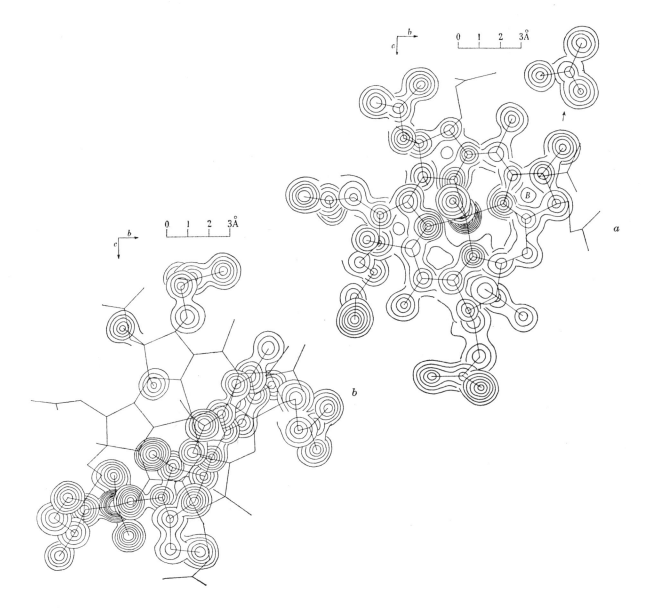

92 · The structure of vitamin B$_{12}$, discovered at Oxford

discovered the value of arts graduates, and have become eager competitors in recruitment. This change is reflected in the great expansion of the work of the University Appointments Committee as a careers advisory service.

In the nineteenth century the boundaries of the different branches of knowledge were assumed to be settled, and specialisation of the Honour Schools was inevitable and fruitful. But in the twentieth century the boundaries are breaking down, and it is probable that the exciting developments will cut across the frontiers of subjects.

The emergence of new Honour Schools since 1919 is a pointer in this direction; those of philosophy, politics and economics, of human geography, of philosophy, physiology and psychology, of economics and engineering (in addition to engineering science). At the same time, the older Honour Schools are constantly evolving, often without a formal change in their structure. For example, an examination paper in philosophy of today would bear little resemblance to a paper in this subject set thirty years ago.

THE TWENTIETH-CENTURY FOUNDATIONS

The renewed vitality of Oxford in the last hundred years has attracted some important benefactions. Since 1945 the building of the science departments has been financed by government grants, though the *University Gazette* regularly records long lists of grants from foundations and firms for research projects. The main field for benefactors remains, as in earlier centuries, the libraries, museums and colleges. The Rockefeller Foundation contributed largely to the building of the New Bodleian building in 1939: and to the Law Library in 1964, to which the Gulbenkian Foundation also contributed.

Nobody could have foreseen the munificent benefactions that came from three men: the obscure son of a clergyman (whose application for entry to Oriel drew from the Provost the remark 'all the Colleges send me their failures'), a bicycle-repairer, a French trader at Aden; respectively, Cecil Rhodes, William Morris Viscount Nuffield, and Antonin Besse. The Rhodes scholars from the Commonwealth and the USA have an increasingly distinguished record of careers in every walk of life: nor must it be overlooked that some of the German Rhodes scholars played an important part in the resistance to Hitler. Lord Nuffield inherited from his yeomen forbears a patriotism for his county of Oxfordshire, and was also by inclination a surgeon *manqué*. His gifts to medicine in Oxford have elevated the Radcliffe Infirmary and its associated hospitals into a great teaching hospital of international significance: his endowment of Nuffield College in 1937 created the first graduate college since the foundation of All Souls. Lord Nuffield at first wanted his college to promote the study of engineering: but he was persuaded by the view of the University that it was unnecessary to duplicate the large school of engineering at Cambridge, and that the immediate need was to expand the social sciences as well as physical chemistry. Hence Nuffield College became an important centre of the social sciences. But it is ironical that within four years of this decision, Britain at war was in desperate need of qualified engineers, and the expansion of engineering at Oxford was put back for a quarter of a century.

The foundation of St Antony's followed that of Nuffield as the second graduate college to be founded in this century, by the benefaction of Monsieur Besse. His attention had been drawn to Oxford by his experience of Oxford graduates whom he had met or employed in the course of his business career. St Antony's College has concentrated on the study of recent history and comparative institutions. Recently the University has promoted the foundation

93   Statue of St John the Baptist (1935) by Eric Gill on the tower of
St John's College

of three more graduate societies, Linacre, St Cross and Iffley. In 1966, it was announced that Iffley College would receive the name of Wolfson College, to record a munificent joint benefaction of over £3,000,000 from the Wolfson Foundation and the Ford Foundation.

Apart from the women's colleges, three men's undergraduate colleges also received their charters in this century. St Edmund Hall and St Peter's College were both promoted from Halls. St Catherine's College arose from St Catherine's Society of non-collegiate students, the graduate element remaining to form Linacre College, and the undergraduate element moving to a new site to form the new St Catherine's College. Its buildings, designed by Arne Jacobsen, are the most remarkable and unified architectural conception of this century in the University. The college owes its rapid creation, not only to the great contributions from industry and the charitable foundations, but to a private American benefactor, Rudolph Light.

EXPANSION AND CHANGE

In various ways the University has resumed in the twentieth century some of the characteristics it possessed in the Middle Ages. It has become again an international University, with the great expansion of graduate students beginning with the Rhodes scholars and visiting scholars from overseas though the bias, in contrast with medieval times, is now oceanic rather than continental. The great migration of scholars from the Nazi régime and other totalitarian régimes before the second world war has stimulated Oxford, and many other universities of the western world, as such migrations often did in the Middle Ages. With the ending of the Anglican monopoly the religious orders have re-established their houses as Private Halls of the University, and some of the Protestant denominations have also established Halls.

The University has regained the position which it lost to the colleges at the end of the Middle Ages. Its budget of £6,000,000 per annum testifies to the activities which it organises and supports. But it would be misleading to suggest that the University and the colleges are two opposed camps. There is interdependence and interpenetration at every level. Most university teachers are also Fellows of colleges, and strenuous efforts are being made to ensure that all established university teachers are provided with fellowships. If in the nineteenth century the University was a loose confederation, it is now a complex federal organism. The role of the colleges does not diminish but increases in importance. Their original function was to create a living community of scholars. This remains an increasingly important function in an expanding university when more and more graduates from other universities are coming to Oxford from all parts of the world, and an increasing proportion of undergraduates are first-generation university students, and lodging space in the centre of an industrial city is becoming scarce. In a university of more than 10,000 members, the colleges provide a means of breaking it down into units of a size and character which can function as living communities.

Hence the colleges are making great efforts to expand both graduate and undergraduate accommodation. Often this has to be done with the help of private benefactors, as government aid for endowment or building is not available, and cannot be expected when other universities are striving to create a residential system with very limited government help.

The colleges provide some safeguard against the danger of 'two cultures'. In the colleges both seniors and juniors pursuing different studies and disciplines are constantly thrown together and are aware of each other's attitudes and problems. In Oxford it was a source of satisfaction, but no great surprise, that one of its Professors of Chemistry was simultaneously President of the Royal Society and President of the Classical Association.

94 Bronze fountain (1962) by Hubert Dalwood. Nuffield College

The colleges also foster a vital form of 'grass-roots' democracy. The youngest Fellows of a college, as members of the governing body, are encouraged and obliged to share constantly in the making of policy decisions affecting the college and the University. If the besetting danger to colleges has been that of an inbred stagnation, their history shows many examples of an active body of Fellows initiating reform. If one cell is inert, there are always others stimulating and revitalising the whole organism.

As in the most vigorous period of the Middle Ages, the University is now drawing on much wider sections of the population, through the financial provision by the State for all students of ability, subject to a parental means test. No country in the western world has made more complete provision for the maintenance of the poor student.

In this century university education has become as important to government and administration as it was in medieval times, when literate and trained minds were essential to the building of civilisation. The scientists have unlocked such vast forces for good and ill that they have become indispensable to government and the economy.

It is therefore unfortunate that the best-known quotation about Oxford is also historically the most misleading. 'Beautiful city! so venerable, so lovely, so unravaged by the fierce intellectual life of our century', wrote Matthew Arnold, 'spreading her gardens to the moonlight, and whispering from her towers the last enchantments of the Middle Ages'. This is an 'ivory-tower' conception of the University, redolent of the romanticism of the nineteenth century. Few, indeed, have failed to fall under the spell of Oxford's 'dreaming spires', but if this

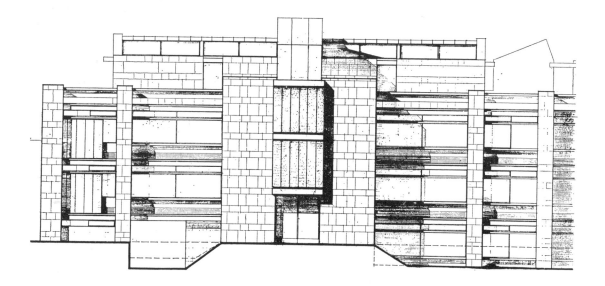

95 Proposed new building by Powell and Moya. Christ Church

96 *(opposite)* Powell and Moya's new building (1961). Brasenose College
97 *(overleaf)* Law Library (1964) by Sir Leslie Martin and C. St J. Wilson

historical survey shows anything it is that Oxford, apart from its moments of slumber, has always reflected and promoted the changing ideals and aspirations of the nation, and the wider community of western civilisation.

Oxford is not a museum of antiquities: the unique quality even of its buildings comes from 'the tide of youthful life that from age to age has flowed through colleges, quadrangle, hall and chamber, through University examination-rooms and Convocation Houses'.

Yet the paradox of all universities is that they can only properly serve the community by pursuing knowledge in their own way. This is a paradox and a problem that governments all over the world have to face and to ponder. Lord Hankey, the wisest civil servant of his generation, who valued more highly than any other of his honours his Fellowship of the Royal Society, understood the nature of university research and education when he used the homely (if somewhat inelegant) phrase, 'We must not kill the goose that lays the golden eggs'. If governments prove to be as wise as many of the great private benefactors of the past, they will do well.

THE FRANKS COMMISSION

The expansion and change of the last sixty years have not been achieved without stress. Three times in this period the University has been the subject of inquiry, one in the form of a Royal Commission, two initiated by the University itself. In 1907 Bishop Gore of Birmingham moved for a Royal Commission in the House of Lords, and complained that Oxford was 'a playground for the sons of the wealthier classes'. Lord Curzon, newly installed as Chancellor of the University, took up the challenge himself, and carried out a one-man commission of inquiry. His 1909 Memorandum to the Vice-Chancellor was an able and constructive document, marred only by a typical Curzonian insensitivity to social trends; he solemnly proposed that a new college should be founded, to be named the 'University Working Man's College'. Fortunately this curious proposal was still-born. His other suggestions, reform of Council and Congregation, the establishment of a General Board of the Faculties, the abolition of compulsory Greek for entrance to the University, and the recognition of women as members of the University were implemented, partly before, or immediately after the war. Meanwhile the decision of the University in 1918 to apply for a government grant necessitated the appointment of the Royal Commission of 1919. It was largely concerned with finance – establishing adequate salaries and pensions in return for the abolition of life-tenure, ensuring the best use of scholarship funds by a means test, keeping down the cost of residence at Oxford. The Commission pointed out that in 1913–14 twenty per cent of scholarship winners came from State day-schools, where the fees were £10 a year or less. The institution of State scholarships to the universities in 1920 could be expected to increase this proportion.

Recently the University has itself appointed a Commission of Inquiry under the chairmanship of Lord Franks, Provost of Worcester College. By 1960 the scale of higher education in Britain had become a political issue. The Crowther Report of 1959 drew attention to the explosive expansion of school sixth forms, and the increasing demand for higher education. The Robbins Committee, appointed by the Prime Minister in 1961 to consider a national system of higher education, was too preoccupied with a vast problem to deal with the position of Oxford in detail, and confessed that they were baffled by the 'obscurity' of Oxford's arrangements and 'the slowness of its decisions'. Oxford itself was not unaware that its machinery of government and finance was no longer adequate, and that it was time for a 'long, hard look' at its purposes and problems.

98   Detail of the Wolfson Building (1964). St Anne's College

The Commission cannot be accused of being unduly inbred. Of its seven members, three were tutorial Fellows of colleges, two were newcomers to Oxford, and two, having started their careers as college Fellows, had subsequently held distinguished posts in government and business. Their report can fairly claim to 'present a picture of the structure and working of a university with a completeness which, we believe, cannot be paralleled'. The Commission also adopted the course, unusual even for a Royal Commission, of making public the written and oral evidence as it was given, in the hope that it would stimulate Oxford 'to a reflective and constructive dialogue within itself'.

The crucial conclusion of the report relates to the size of the University. It reaffirms the distinctive character of Oxford as a collegiate university. It follows from this and from the geography of the city that Oxford should remain a medium-sized university, growing from the present ten thousand to thirteen thousand over the next twenty years. And most of this growth should be in graduate students. With the planned expansion of other universities, there is no longer the pressure, as there was in the twenty years after the war, to increase its undergraduate population. But Oxford, with its immense library and teaching resources, its international status, has a 'manifest destiny' to undertake a large share of the expansion of graduate studies.

A great deal of the report is necessarily concerned with highly technical matters of structure, finance and machinery of government, which only dons and administrators will relish. Their proposals aim at speeding up the process of decision, strengthening the co-operation between colleges and between the colleges and the University, and improving the finances of the poorer colleges. But it preserves throughout a remarkably coherent philosophy of education, and does not overlook the fact that the essence of the University, as it was in the beginning, consists of scholars exploring the frontiers of knowledge, who are also imparting their knowledge to generations of students. Everything else is ancillary.

The report reaffirms emphatically the value of the Oxford tutorial system, based on the weekly essay and the weekly hour individually with the tutor, as it was evolved by the great tutors of the nineteenth century, such as Jowett. 'At its heart is a theory of teaching young men and women to think for themselves'. But the Commission were perturbed by signs that the real value of the tutorial was being undermined by the pressures caused by the expansion of knowledge and the overloading of the undergraduate syllabus. The tutorial could easily be misused to become another and wasteful form of imparting information. The Commission has therefore made recommendations for restoring a proper balance between lectures, seminars and tutorials, and reviewing the syllabus of the Honour Schools.

The Commission found that forty per cent of applicants awarded entrance scholarships came from State-maintained schools, as compared with the figure of twenty per cent reported by the 1919 Commission. Moreover forty per cent of all entrants to the University now came from such schools. But the Commission drew the conclusion that this proportion was still too low, and recommended that Oxford should intensify its efforts to make contact with the two thousand schools in this category to attract more such applicants, and to adapt its entrance examination for candidates who had spent two, rather than, three years in a school sixth form.

Some but not all of its recommendations have been adopted. The poorer Colleges now receive the proceeds of University taxation of the richer Colleges to strengthen their finances. The central administration has been strengthened and streamlined. There is now a full-time Vice-Chancellor for four years, and the office is elective instead of being confined to Heads of Houses in order of seniority. So far the change is not startling as the choice has fallen on

99 River Building (1964) by Arne Jacobsen. St Catherine's College

Heads of Houses. The admissions system is being continuously adapted to meet the changing educational structure of the country.

The wave of student militancy which spread from the U.S.A. to the European universities in the late 1960s had little impact on Oxford, largely owing to the humanising effect of the strong collegiate structure. But student participation in College and University matters has markedly increased. After much debate Oxford followed the Cambridge example and admitted a limited number of women undergraduates to five of the men's Colleges. This change, which is unlikely to stand still, has been absorbed without ado.

In the 1970s, financial restriction imposes a period of consolidation and pause, in contrast to the rapid expansion of the 1960s.

100   The new Engineering Laboratory (1963)

Notes on Illustrations

1 VAULTING OVER THE PRESBYTERY OF THE CATHEDRAL. CHRIST CHURCH

The lierne stone vaulting over the presbytery of the Cathedral may be compared with the vaulting of the Divinity School in its energy and intricacy. It dates from the late fifteenth century and so from one of the last generations of the Austin Canons whose priory of St Frideswide was suppressed in April 1524 to enrich Cardinal Wolsey's new college. Less fortunate than the vaulting are the alterations to the east end undertaken by Sir George Gilbert Scott (1811–78) in 1870–1. He introduced the rose window, the arcading, and the two pseudo-Norman windows below, and so displaced the former, and doubtless more fitting, fourteenth-century decorated window.

2 THE ADORATION OF THE MAGI; DETAIL OF THE TAPESTRY BY SIR EDWARD BURNE-JONES AND WILLIAM MORRIS. EXETER COLLEGE CHAPEL

In 1927 the tapestry of *The Adoration of the Magi*, hanging on the south side of Sir George Gilbert Scott's chapel (1845–9) of Exeter College, was still considered to be one of the sights of Oxford. Designed by Sir Edward Burne-Jones Bt (1833–98) and executed by William Morris (1834–96) at the looms at Merton Abbey, it was presented by them in 1890. In view of the failure of the decorations done for the Union Society Library in 1858, in which both artists collaborated with D.G.Rossetti, Arthur Hughes and Val Prinsep, this tapestry is a reminder of Burne-Jones and Morris' first meeting as undergraduates at Exeter College in 1852. The subject proved a popular one. A comparable tapestry was given to Eton College Chapel in 1895 and Ambrose Poynter unsuccessfully proposed the subject in 1903 for the centrepiece of the Chapel of King's College, Cambridge. It was one of the numerous, indeed perennial, designs for that high altar. The cartoon for the tapestry was presented to the Victoria and Albert Museum.

3 BISHOP FOX'S STANDING SALT. CORPUS CHRISTI COLLEGE

Corpus Christi College was, and is, particularly fortunate in succeeding in preserving its college plate from melting down when the Oxford mint was active between 1642 and 1646. In the hexagonal gilt standing salt and cover the college still possesses, with a number of other pieces, an original gift of its founder, Bishop Richard Fox. Resembling an hour glass in shape, the twelve panels on the base and six on the cover are filled with open-work tracery with hares and hounds and a pelican. Around the base of both salt and cover is a band bearing the pattern of a pelican between the initials Rd (for Ricardus Dunelm i.e. Durham).

The Founder of Corpus Christi College, Richard Fox (1448–1528), held successively the sees of Exeter 1487, Bath and Wells 1492, Durham 1494, and Winchester 1501. Fox was an influential statesman during the reign of Henry VII and the early years of Henry VIII's. Among the offices which he held were Secretary of State and Lord Privy Seal and he also acted as a Chief Diplomatic Envoy. In 1500 Fox was appointed Chancellor of Cambridge University and he was Master of Pembroke College, Cambridge 1507–19. He founded Corpus Christi College at Oxford in 1517.

4 'FOUNDER'S CUP' AND MAZER. ORIEL COLLEGE

In 1493 the Oriel College Treasurer's accounts record the purchase for £4.18.1 of this silver-gilt beaker and cover, which a hundred years later was described as 'the founders cupp double guilded with a cheine of SS and E and six crownes on the outside ...' The golden chain was the cognizance of the House of Lancaster apparently devised by Henry IV before his accession. The date of the beaker is not certain but it is now known to have been made in Paris and probably decorated for Prince Edward, son of Henry VI and Margaret of Anjou between 1462 and 1471. Thus, although a century and more later than the foundation of the college by Adam de Brome and Edward II in 1326, the beaker remains a notable piece of plate.

The maplewood mazer with silver-gilt mounts is said to have been given to the college by John Carpenter, the Provost from 1430 and Bishop of Worcester from 1443 until his death in 1476.

5 ROCK CRYSTAL SALT. TRINITY COLLEGE

Sir Bernard Eckstein bequeathed the rock crystal standing salt to his former college in 1948 together with other notable pieces of plate, demonstrating the continuing tradition of generosity by which colleges and the University are enriched. The salt is dated 1549 but the maker's mark has not been identified. The stem consists of a cylinder of rock crystal which encloses a draped female figure standing on a pedestal. To the Ashmolean Museum Sir Bernard bequeathed a fine collection of English glasses and a group of porcelain of superlative quality from the Vincennes and Vienna factories.

6 GREAT QUADRANGLE TO THE NORTH-EAST. MAGDALEN COLLEGE

The building of the boundary walls of Magdalen College, founded by William of Waynflete in 1458, did not begin until 1467 (see also no. 39). The site purchased for the college was that of the former Hospital of St John the Evangelist. The foundation of the chapel was blessed in 1474 and the building of the Founder's Tower and the Great Quadrangle with its cloister seems then to have made rapid progress and to have been largely completed by 1483. Much of the stone came from the quarries at Headington although stone was also obtained from the Abbot of Bruern's quarry at Milton, from Taynton and from Wheatley. The work was directed by William Orchard, 'freemason of Oxford' to whom a lease of one of the Headington quarries was granted and who acted as mason, contractor and architect.

7 THE ALFRED JEWEL, FRONT AND BACK. ASHMOLEAN MUSEUM

King Alfred's Jewel was found at Newton Park near Athelney in 1693 and was bequeathed to the University by Colonel Nathaniel Palmer in 1717. The front of the jewel is made of gold with cloisonné enamel beneath rock crystal while the back is richly engraved with a floral design. Round the edge is the inscription – AELFRED MEC HEHT GEWYRCAN – (Aelfred ordered me to be made). At the base is a boar's head with a hollow snout. Although the use of the jewel is not certain, its beauty, the inscription and place of discovery strongly suggest that it belonged to Alfred the Great (871–901).

8 SILVER PENNIES OF AETHELRED II AND WILLIAM I, MINTED IN OXFORD. HEBERDEN COIN ROOM, ASHMOLEAN MUSEUM
From the reign of Alfred until 1279, the Oxford mint and its moneyers produced a succession of silver pennies. The penny, the obverse and reverse of which are reproduced above, dates from the reign of Aethelred II (976–1016) and also bears the name of the moneyer Aethelmaer. The penny below is from the reign of the first of the Norman Kings, William I (1066–87).

These coins, like those of Charles I which date from the brief revival of the Oxford mint during the Civil War, are preserved in the Heberden Coin Room in the Ashmolean Museum and form part of a collection which is one of the richest and oldest in England. It should be noted that the pennies are here reproduced a third to a half larger than their actual size.

9 WHALE FROM AN ENGLISH BESTIARY. BODLEIAN LIBRARY, MS ASHMOLE 1511, FOL. 86v
This whale is one of the illustrations to a Bestiary decorated in England in the late twelfth century. The book consists of one hundred and five leaves of vellum. The whale comes at the beginning of the section devoted to fish, headed 'Incipit de piscibus. *Pisces dicti unde et pecus, a pescendo*'. The other sections on animals, birds, bees and trees are equally richly and vividly illustrated. The small folio manuscript was among the extensive collection of manuscripts and the greater part of his library of printed books, 1,758 volumes in all, bequeathed to the University by Elias Ashmole in 1692 (see also no. 56).

10 THE 'BRASENNOSE'; BRONZE DOOR-KNOCKER. BRASENOSE COLLEGE
In the account of the buildings of Brasenose College given in volume III of the Victoria History of the County of Oxford, published in 1954, there is given as just and amusing an history of the 'eponymous totem', the Brazen Nose, which can now be seen in the college hall, as is likely to be established: 'An old house at Stamford, known as Brazen Nose, was for sale in 1890. Its name was certainly three centuries old, for when Twyne visited the town in 1617, he noticed four old houses which he thought might have been academic halls at the time of the migration of 1333 [see p. 21]: of these, one was known as Black Hall, another as Brasenose Hall; and in a record of 1335 there is mention of Brasenose at Stamford. It was suggested to the college that in 1333 some scholars from the Hall had stolen the handle from the door of Brasenose Hall in Oxford, which at that time belonged to University College, and affixed it to the lodging which they found in Stamford. This hypothesis was not unreasonable; the college was therefore persuaded to buy the property: the Nose was brought to Oxford in 1890 with much honour, but the house in Stamford was sold in 1932.'

11 SOUTH DOOR OF THE CHURCH OF ST PETER IN THE EAST
After centuries of service from about 1150 the church of St Peter's in the East was deconsecrated in 1966. The use, but not the freehold, of the church has been transferred to St Edmund Hall for adaptation as a much-needed library for the college. Although the cost of preserving the fabric is high, it is hoped that the library will eventually be installed without detracting from the Norman and later architecture. The parochial responsibilities of St Peter's have been undertaken by the parish of St Mary the Virgin and a number of the church's plain but impressive silver-gilt cups have been deposited on loan at the Ashmolean Museum.

12 ST FRIDESWIDE; WINDOW IN THE LATIN CHAPEL OF THE CATHEDRAL. CHRIST CHURCH
One of the fourteenth-century windows in the Latin Chapel of the Cathedral represents St Frideswide, a Saxon nun who founded a Christian church and nunnery on the site of the present cathedral before her death in about 735. Although St Frideswide's foundation was small and did not long survive her death, she remains the patron saint of the cathedral and of the diocese of Oxford, and the place of her shrine in the Lady Chapel is still venerated.

13 PLATO AND SOCRATES, FROM A TREATISE ON ASTRONOMY. BODLEIAN LIBRARY, MS ASHMOLE 304
Socrates writing with Plato standing behind him is drawn in a book of astronomical tables and prognostications. It is in the style of the school of St Albans under Matthew Paris, and is partly coloured in green and blue; the names are inscribed in red.

The volume in which this illustration is to be found was inscribed by Edward Lhuyd (1660–1709), who succeeded Dr Robert Plot when he retired from the Keepership of the Ashmolean Museum early in 1691, 'Ex dono – Vaughan Coll. Aen Nasi schol'. It has been presumed that it must have been put into Ashmole's collection here to fill a gap caused by the early loss of Ashmole's own manuscripts 304 and 305. Ashmole's bequest of his books was made to the Museum which bears his name and not transferred to the care of the Bodleian Library until a later period.

14 BASTION IN THE CITY WALL. NEW COLLEGE
One of the conditions of the Royal Grant (of 1379) of permission for the building of New College on its site in the north-east corner of the city was that the college should undertake to keep the defensive wall in good repair. As a result of this condition the wall is now best preserved, and therefore can be seen to best advantage, in New College. The north-east bastion, a photograph of which is reproduced here, has arrow slits at ground level and above for the protection of the approaches to the wall. The east and north tract of the wall now enclose the garden of New College. On its north side it provides shelter for a fine border of shrubs and herbaceous plants. The foundation stone of New College was laid on 5 March 1380 and the buildings were probably completed by 14 April 1386.

15 INTERIOR OF MERTON COLLEGE LIBRARY
John Bloxham, Warden of Merton College from 1375 until 1387, has been described as the 'presiding genius' of the library, which was built between 1373 and 1378. William Humbertyle was the principal mason and both he and Bloxham travelled to see other libraries. The bookcases shown in this view were introduced in the sixteenth century and were probably the model for those Bodley fitted in Duke Humphrey's library (see no. 25) at about the same time. The medieval bookcases or lecterns were doubtless also arranged in bays with fittings to take the chained books. The library forms the south side of Mob Quad, previously known, perhaps more suitably, as Bachelor's Quad.

16 FOUNDER'S CUP. THE QUEEN'S COLLEGE
The silver-gilt buffalo-horn loving cup is reputed to have been given to the Queen's College by Robert of Eglesfield (d. 1349), chaplain to Queen Philippa of Hainault, wife of Edward III, to whose patronage Eglesfield commended the Collegiate Hall. The gold lip is inscribed WACCEYL (Wassail) and the eagle on the lid makes a punning allusion to the founder.

17 PAGE OF A MANUSCRIPT OF ARISTOTLE. BALLIOL COLLEGE, MS 232B
From the conjunction of the coats-of-arms of the Moels and Pomeroy families which are painted in this copy of Aristotle it is likely that it belonged to John Pomeroy, rector of Aveton Giffard, who was granted a year's dispensation from his parochial duties to study in Oxford in 1349. The book, with its occasional drawings of monsters and fantastic beasts, was probably written in Oxford at this time. How it came to Balliol is not known, but it was there before the close of the fourteenth century. 'By far the finest, as well as the largest, private collection to survive in England from the Middle Ages' is the description given to the surviving half of the library of medieval Balliol which was given or bequeathed to the college by William

Grey (d. 1478), Chancellor of the University and Bishop of Ely. Not later than 1431 Grey was a 'sojourner' at Balliol and there began his collection of books. He studied in Cologne and in Florence and also enabled John Free, the humanist writer, to study in Italy.

18 THE VIRGIN AND CHILD; GLASS IN THE EAST WINDOW OF MERTON COLLEGE CHAPEL

The stained glass in Merton Chapel is particularly remarkable both for the original panels of *c.* 1300 *in situ* in fourteen side-windows of the choir and in the intricate tracery of the east window, and for the fifteenth-century panels in the east window. The subject of the Virgin appears four times in glass of the chapel, a fact no doubt explained by the joint dedication of the chapel to the Virgin and St John the Baptist. The delicately coloured Virgin and Child which is reproduced here is set in the central light of the great east windows above the altar.

19 HEAD OF A BISHOP FROM THE CHURCH OF ST MARY THE VIRGIN. NEW COLLEGE CLOISTER

In the cloister of New College there now stand, together with a fire engine of 1760, eight statues which become their surroundings. A further group are in the second quadrangle of All Souls. These much weathered figures originally stood in the niches on the tower of St Mary's, the University Church, which was built in the 1280s. The spire was added about 1320. In 1893, Sir Thomas Graham Jackson was called in to inspect the fabric and the statues; the latter were found to be decayed and insecure, and so were taken down and replaced by modern copies. They were then set up in the lower storey of the old Congregation House. The restoration of the tower was completed by 1896 and the statues remained in the Congregation House until the mid 1950s when the late Warden of New College, A.H. Smith, moved the eight statues to his college, where they can now be seen.

20 WILLIAM OF WYKEHAM'S CROZIER. NEW COLLEGE

A comparison of the pastoral staffs of William of Wykeham and Richard Fox (no. 33) shows at once that the kneeling figure of a bishop in the circle of the former must once have been supported by other decorative features. The inset panels of translucent enamel also contrast with the more formalised pattern used on the crook of Fox's crozier. Having fallen into disrepair during the Reformation, it was restored in 1753, according to the history of the college, and is now housed in a specially prepared recess on the north side of the chancel. A posthumous portrait of William of Wykeham confronts the crozier on the south side. William of Wykeham (1324–1404) bequeathed to his college not only his crozier but also his mitre, dalmatics and sandals.

21 LION AND PELICAN; FIGURES CROWNING BUTTRESSES ON THE WEST CLOISTER IN THE GREAT QUADRANGLE. MAGDALEN COLLEGE

In 1508–9 the accounts for the cloister of Magdalen College record the expenditure of more than £12 on 'gargels', probably 'the curious figures' on each buttress on the east, north and west sides of the cloister. John Butt, stoneworker, and Robert Carver were paid for 'le gargels' they had made and payment for erecting them was made to Richard Heys, Richard Lewis, William Symsell, Richard Bennett and Henry Fostar. The two creatures reproduced here from the south-west corner, are a lion and a pelican vulning herself (see no. 33). Among the many others are mythical beasts as well as human figures. The result suggests a medieval Bestiary illustrated not in a manuscript but in stone.

22 STATUE OF THE VIRGIN. MERTON COLLEGE CHAPEL

As remarked earlier, Merton College Chapel is dedicated to the Blessed Virgin Mary and St John the Baptist, and their statues stand in niches on the exterior of the north transept facing onto Merton Street, the Virgin on the right, St John on the left. While the south transept was completed about 1367, the north transept dates from 1419–25. The statues are presumably contemporary; that of the Virgin, despite the damage it has sustained over the years, is both comely and graceful.

23 EAST RANGE OF THE FRONT QUADRANGLE. ALL SOULS COLLEGE

By the end of the seventeenth century the front quadrangle of All Souls had become too small for the needs of the Fellows. Both Dr George Clarke and Nicholas Hawksmoor made plans for the enlarging and realigning of the quadrangle. A central covered way was to connect a new entrance to the proposed hall and chapel and replace the still surviving east range. The fortunate survival of the original buildings provides an excellent example of a fifteenth-century quadrangle. Built by Richard Chevynton and Robert Janyns, the quadrangle consists of only two storeys. The stairs go straight and steeply up with a pair of rooms on each side on each floor. The construction was accomplished between the foundation of the college by Henry VI and Henry Chichele, Archbishop of Canterbury, in 1438, and 1443 when the college was endowed and its statutes issued.

24 VAULTING OVER THE DIVINITY SCHOOL. BODLEIAN LIBRARY

As early as 1423 the University was seeking contributions for the Divinity School, and in 1427 work had begun on land acquired from Balliol College. The work proceeded unevenly. Cardinal Beaufort's legacy of five hundred marks resulted in a period of activity between 1448 and 1453, but it was not until 1483 that the lovely fan vaulting of the roof was finished. The early building was in the care of the master mason Richard Winchcombe, who had worked for New College between 1408 and 1418, and it is probable that the completion was entrusted to William Orchard, who was responsible for the building of the Great Quadrangle at Magdalen.

25 DUKE HUMPHREY'S LIBRARY. BODLEIAN LIBRARY

The view of Duke Humphrey's Library is taken from the Art's End looking west to the window in the Selden End. With the completion of the fan vaulting of the roof of the Divinity School in 1483 and the upper storey by 1490, the building could be used for housing the books given to the University by Humphrey, Duke of Gloucester (1391–1447) from 1411 onwards. Whether as a result of the Visitations or absence of supervision and endowment, the library fell into disorder in the sixteenth century. In a letter of 23 February 1598 Sir Thomas Bodley announced his intention of restoring and refitting the library and in March Bodley and Sir Henry Savile discussed the subject. The timber was acquired from Merton College as also was the principle on which the bookcases were arranged, being set in bays. When the floor of the library had to be renewed recently the marks on the walls showed where the fifteenth-century lectern presses had stood. In their place Bodley set up the three-decker presses which are still in use. The library was nearly completed by June 1600 but was not opened until November 1602. The painted panels of the ceiling bear the arms and motto of the University.

26 SOUTH DOORWAY OF ST MARY'S CHAPEL. HERTFORD COLLEGE

Over the doorway to the former octagonal chapel of St Mary stands a stone relief divided into compartments, in the outside of which can be seen the Virgin and the Angel of the Annunciation. The chapel, correctly that of Our Lady at Smith Gate, existed as the Octagon Bookshop until after the First World War and was then altered and restored in 1931 to form a lodge for the new buildings of Hertford College. According to Anthony Wood the chapel was built 'as tis said by one Whobberdie or de Hyberdine' about 1521. If the relief dates from this period, as well it may, it is further evidence of the retardatory character of building in Oxford.

27 BERNARD VAN ORLEY, CHRIST BEARING THE CROSS; DETAIL OF AN ALTARPIECE. ORIEL COLLEGE

This detail is taken from the painting of *Christ Bearing the Cross* by Bernard van Orley (1491/2–1542). It was presented to Oriel College in 1911 by Alfred Stowe, Fellow of Wadham, in memory of his brother, William Henry Stowe, once a Fellow of Oriel, who died at Balaclava in 1855, and for several years it was hung in the college chapel. The companion to this, *The Crown of Thorns*, was in the same collection and a third painting, *Christ resting on the way to Golgotha*, belonging to the same altarpiece, is now in the Scottish National Gallery. On the back of the painting in Oriel are two coats-of-arms which have been identified as those of Henry III, Count of Nassau, and his third wife Marcia de Mendoza. From 1518 van Orley was court painter to Margaret of Austria, in whose court the first prince of the House of Orange, Henry of Nassau, was tutor to Charles V. The fallen Christ occupies the centre of the panel to the left of the detail reproduced here. In the background is a typically Flemish landscape.

28 THE GIANT SALT. ALL SOULS COLLEGE

The fifteenth-century Giant, or Huntsman, Salt was given to All Souls College in 1799 by Mrs Catherine Griffiths. The crystal bowl and cover are enclosed by silver-gilt mounts and are supported by a stem in the form of a bearded huntsman, who appears giant-like in relation to the activity about his feet, where a huntsman can be seen encouraging hounds. The colouring given to this standing salt is unusual: the finial is painted green, the face and hands of the 'giant' are coloured and so is the base. There is good reason to believe that this colouration is authentic and dates from the fifteenth century.

29 EIGHT SIGNS OF THE ZODIAC; CARVED BOSSES FROM THE FITZJAMES GATEHOUSE. MERTON COLLEGE

The gateway to the east of the hall formed part of the new lodgings for the Warden of Merton College, built by Warden Fitzjames in 1497. Unusually, the date of the commencement can be fixed precisely, because Fitzjames, with a foresight of which Elias Ashmole would have approved, had a horoscope cast for his new house. The foundation stone was laid at 10.20 a.m. on Monday, 12 March 1497, and it is not surprising that the vault of the gateway was decorated with the signs of the zodiac. Such a subject also befits a college which was remarkable from its early days for its mathematicians and scientists. The gateway now gives onto the Fellow's Quadrangle built between 1608 and 1610 through the initiative of Sir Henry Savile, Warden from 1585 to 1621.

30 DETAIL FROM A FLEMISH TAPESTRY SHOWING THE BETROTHAL OF PRINCE ARTHUR AND CATHARINE OF ARAGON. MAGDALEN COLLEGE

When the *Treasures of Oxford* exhibition was held at the Goldsmith's Hall in London to mark the Coronation in 1953, one of the group of tapestries which now hang in the Founder's Tower at Magdalen College was shown. The set of tapestries, from which this detail of the Betrothal is taken, are thought to be associated with Catharine of Aragon. Richard Mayew, the President of the college from 1480 to 1506, was one of the envoys to meet the Spanish Princess when she reached England in 1501 for her marriage on 14 November to Prince Arthur. Unfortunately the provenance of the tapestries does not help to elucidate their history, since the college records concerning them go back no earlier than the middle of the last century.

31 CARDINAL WOLSEY'S DIAL AND ARCHBISHOP LAUD'S CLOG ALMANACK. MUSEUM OF THE HISTORY OF SCIENCE

Both these scientific instruments are associated with eminent Princes of the Church, each of whom took a close interest in the University. In the case of Archbishop William Laud, whose wooden almanack is opened like a fan, it can be argued that his interest was too all-embracing. Laud gave the almanack to the Bodleian Library in 1636.

The polyhedral dial was given to the University by Dr Lewis Evans in 1924. Of gilt brass, it was in all probability made by Nicholas Kratzer (1486–1556), astronomer and horologer to Henry VIII and a member of Corpus Christi College. The dial bears on its base the arms of Cardinal Wolsey (?1475–1530, Fellow of Magdalen College 1497) and those of York Minster of which see Wolsey

became Archbishop in 1518. The dial can therefore be dated between that year and the date of Wolsey's death in 1530.

32 BISHOP FOX'S CHALICE. CORPUS CHRISTI COLLEGE

Bishop Richard Fox's chalice is the third piece of plate reproduced here which is associated personally with the founder of Corpus Christi College (see nos. 3 and 33). Again it is not known whether the gold chalice and its paten were given or bequeathed to the college by Fox. Unlike the salt and the crozier it can be precisely dated, since it bears the London hall marks for 1507. The figures engraved beneath the delineated tracery in the six compartments of the foot are the Crucifixion, the Virgin and Child, St Mary Magdalen, St Jerome, St Margaret and St Augustine. At the top and bottom of the knop are carved tracery compartments and in the centre are six raised facets decorated with red and green enamel.

33 BISHOP FOX'S CROZIER. CORPUS CHRISTI COLLEGE

Bishop Fox is thought to have bequeathed his pastoral staff to the college he founded in 1517. Within the circle of the crozier can be seen the representation of St Peter, the patron saint of Exeter Cathedral (Fox was bishop of Exeter from 1487 to 1492). The inlaid pattern running round the upper part of the crook is of roses and pelicans on a black enamel ground and the pelican in her piety is again represented below the winged angel. Few, if any, objects from before 1500 carry as strong an association with their owners as the croziers of Bishop Fox and William of Wykeham (no. 20), both founders of colleges.

The motif of the pelican is incorporated in the college crest (Azure, a pelican with wings endorsed, vulning herself). The emblem, a common one in the Middle Ages, and employed by St Thomas Aquinas and Dante, recalls the crucified Christ giving His blood for mankind, just as the pelican was thought to shed hers for her children.

34 QUADRANGLE OF ST EDMUND HALL

The small quadrangle of St Edmund Hall has an individual charm which befits the last and longest lived of the halls of residence established in the Middle Ages. Described as *Aula Sti Edmundi* in a rent roll of Oseney Abbey of 1317, the messuage has been in existence since before 1238. The buildings illustrated here date from a much later period; the range to the left is of the sixteenth century and at the east end of the quadrangle are the former library and the chapel built by William Bird (1624–after 1683) between 1680 and 1682 and completed by Bartholomew Peisley the elder (c. 1620–94) in 1685–6. This building was initiated by Stephen Penton (Principal 1675–84).

The arrangement of the library is interesting in that it may be considered a prototype of the design commonly used in the eighteenth century. The open central area with a gallery antedates by several years the library at Queen's, which still followed the medieval precedent of Merton College Library, also followed in the refitting of Duke Humphrey's Library, whereby the bookcases are arranged in bays set at right angles to the walls.

35 EAST RANGE OF THE GREAT QUADRANGLE. CHRIST CHURCH

Mercury is the name which has been given to the ornamental pool in the foreground of the illustration, after the statue which stands in the centre. The first statue of Mercury was made by William Bird in 1670 at Canon Richard Gardiner's expense; the second with a bronze head and a lead body was given to the House by Anthony Radcliffe, the chief benefactor of Peckwater Quadrangle, and was damaged in 1817. After more than a hundred years Tom Quad was once again given a centre-piece by Mr. H.B.Bompas in 1928. The present copy, in lead, of Mercury by Giovanni da Bologna stands on a pedestal designed for it by Sir Edwin Lutyens.

Reflected in Mercury is the shortened spire of the Cathedral, restored between 1870 and 1872 by Sir George Gilbert Scott. Beyond is part of the south-east range of Cardinal College (1525–9), like part of the west range and the hall, completed in Wolsey's lifetime by the master-masons Thomas Redman (or Redmayne) and John Lubyns (or Lovyns). Despite Dean Samuel Fell's attempt before the Civil War, the north side was not completed until the tenure of his son John Fell, Dean from 1660–86. The arches on the ground storey form the wall arcade from which the stone vault of the intended cloister would have sprung. Although this huge cloister was never built, the arcading continues all round the completed Great Quadrangle.

36 ST JOHN THE BAPTIST AND ST MARY MAGDALEN; CARVED PANEL ON THE WEST WALL OF THE HALL. MAGDALEN COLLEGE

The hall of Magdalen College was begun in 1474. The linenfold panelling which covers the walls was bought in London, shipped up the Thames to Henley and then brought overland to the college. Behind the high table the panelling is enriched by a series of carved and painted panels. The centre group of nine is twice inscribed 1541. At its centre is a portrait of Henry VIII flanked by scenes from the life of Christ and St Mary Magdalen. Suitably for a hall, the three upper panels show the Anointing of Christ's Feet, the Supper at Emmaus and the Last Supper. On each side of the central group is a smaller one consisting of four panels, two of which bear coats-of-arms. Along the top of the panelling behind the high table runs a similarly carved and attractively coloured frieze.

37 WADHAM COLLEGE HALL

£11,360 was the cost of building Wadham College, quadrangle, chapel, hall, library fittings and plate all included. The building was rapidly accomplished in three years and five months between 1610 and 1613. Work began on the roof of the hall in 1612 and in the summer of the same year John Bolton was at work on the screen. For this and the chapel screen he received £82 at the end of June 1613. Mrs Wadham's representatives inspected the college in March 1613 and the first members were admitted in April. Thus the college was built not only over an unusually brief period but also with an equal degree of consistency and symmetry. Deservedly, a medal consisting of their portraits was cast to commemorate Nicholas and Dorothy Wadham and an example is preserved in the Heberden Coin Room in the Ashmolean Museum.

38 VAULT OF THE GREAT STAIRCASE. CHRIST CHURCH

According to Sir John Peshall, Dr Samuel Fell, Dean of Christ Church from 1638 until his displacement in 1648, was responsible for the building of the staircase to the hall 'as it now is, by the help of – Smith, an artificer from London – and built the most exquisite Arch, that now is.' It has been suggested that the Smith who worked on the vaulting may be identical with the John Smith who worked on the great gate of Trinity College, Cambridge.

In 1805 the staircase was designed by James Wyatt in his Gothic style suitably attuned to the late flowering of the perpendicular Gothic of the vaulting. Externally, the staircase is now surmounted by the 'pseudo-Tudor Belfry Tower' built to the designs of George Frederick Bodley (1827–1907) between 1876 and 1879.

39 THE OLD GRAMMAR HALL. MAGDALEN COLLEGE

The Grammar Hall, one of the few buildings in Oxford as yet un-refaced and unrestored after the activity of the last ten years, is a reminder to the visitor emerging from the entrance of the chapel and cloister of Magdalen of what many of the buildings of Oxford looked like up to 1956 – flaking, crumbling, blackened, gnarled and decayed. In Oxford it can scarcely be considered a paradox that one of the oldest looking buildings is, in fact, relatively young, dating as it does from about 1614. It was restored and adapted by John Chessell Buckler (1798–1894). Magdalen College was founded by William of Waynflete (1395–1486) in 1458, ten years after his foundation of Magdalen Hall. Waynflete was successively Master of Winchester (1429–42), Provost of Eton from 1443, Bishop of Winchester and Lord High Chancellor of England. The free Grammar School at Magdalen was founded in 1480, shortly before Waynflete's death, just outside the college gates. The work was committed to the charge of Richard Bernes and probably completed by 1483. Waynflete's school was modelled on the relationship established by William of Wykeham between his two foundations, Winchester and New College, the school providing the college with well-grounded scholars.

40 PORTRAIT OF QUEEN ELIZABETH I. JESUS COLLEGE

Of the three portraits of Queen Elizabeth in the possession of Jesus College two may lay claim to be considered contemporary. One of these, inscribed 1590, hangs over the high table in the college hall. In it the Queen is shown in an elaborately patterned dress with the addition of such naturalistic details as an heartsease pansy, wild strawberries, cherries and a thistle. Queen Elizabeth I issued the letters patent for the foundation of Jesus College on 27 June 1571 at the petition of Dr Hugh Price (c. 1495–1574).

41 MONUMENT TO SIR HENRY SAVILE. MERTON COLLEGE CHAPEL

The monument to Sir Henry Savile (1549–1622, Brasenose College and Fellow and Warden of Merton College) in the south transept of Merton College Chapel balances that to Savile's friend Sir Thomas Bodley in the north transept. From left to right the figures on the monument are St Chrysostom, Ptolemy, Euclid and Tacitus. They symbolise Savile's scholarly achievements. In 1570 he read 'his ordinaries in the Almagest of Ptolemy' and his translation of four books of the Histories of Tacitus appeared in 1591. His greatest endeavour was the edition of St Chrysostom for the printing of which he had hoped to obtain the Royal French Type. Instead he engaged the King's printer, John Norton, and supervised the publication at Eton where he had been appointed Provost in 1596. The eight folio volumes appeared between 1610 and 1613. In 1621 was published Savile's *Praelectiones tresdecim in principium elementorum Euclidis*. Both Merton and Eton are depicted on the base of the monument.

42 CENTRAL FEATURE OF THE WEST RANGE OF CANTERBURY QUADRANGLE WITH STATUE OF QUEEN HENRIETTA MARIA. ST JOHN'S COLLEGE

Archbishop Laud commissioned the two bronze statues of Charles I and Henrietta Maria from Hubert le Sueur (1580–1670) for £400 in May 1633. In their niches the statues form the central focal points of the east and west ranges of Canterbury Quadrangle. The ornate settings were carved by Nicholas Stone's two assistants, Anthony Gore and Henry Acres. The grotesques and the cartouches were carved by Acres. Although the lion and the unicorn are awkwardly cramped in the partially broken pediment, the other sculptural adjuncts are not inharmonious. The Canterbury Quadrangle, chiefly due to the initiative of Archbishop Laud (1573–1645), who had been President of St John's College from 1611 to 1621, was completed between 1632 and 1636.

43 THE TEMPTATION OF ADAM AND EVE; STAINED-GLASS WINDOW BY ABRAHAM VAN LINGE. UNIVERSITY COLLEGE CHAPEL

The tree under which Adam and Eve are being tempted belongs to a similar genus as that under which Jonah is surveying Nineveh in the window at the west end of the north aisle of the Cathedral. The Flemish artist, Abraham van Linge, has, however, differentiated between the fruits. The first window on the south side of University College Chapel shows not only the Temptation but in the background the expulsion of Adam and Eve from Paradise. It is signed ABRAHAM VAN/LINGE FECIT 1641 and above the signature are depicted a camel and a unicorn. Of the nine windows, one of which is in the antechapel, seven depict scenes from the Old Testament and two illustrate incidents in the New Testament. The most dramatic is on the north side nearest the altar and represents Jonah being disgorged by the Whale. Van Linge has successfully painted shipping and a port beyond (i.e. above) the subject (see also no. 46).

44 MONUMENT TO SIR THOMAS BODLEY. BODLEIAN LIBRARY

The bust of Sir Thomas Bodley (1545–1613, Magdalen College and Fellow of Merton College) stands on the left of the entrance to Duke Humphrey's Library. It was given to the University in 1605, in the sitter's lifetime, by Thomas Sackville, Earl of Dorset, K.G. (1536–

1608, Chancellor of the University from 1591 until his death) 'for the perpetual memory' of the founder, Bodley, and Lord Dorset 'sent it, carved to the life by an excellent hand at London'. Bodley had also been active in restoring and reviving Duke Humphrey's Library which had been despoiled in the Visitation of Edward VI. This bust has been considered the best surviving portrait of Bodley. It is superior to the bust on his monument in the antechapel of Merton College which is surrounded by allegorical figures of Grammar, Rhetoric, Music and Arithmetic, reminiscent of the School of Fontainebleau. Nicholas Stone recorded in his Notebook that 'In May 1615 I did set up a Tombe for Sir Thomas Bodley' and that he was paid '100 £ of good mony'.

45 THE SUPPER AT EMMAUS (DETAIL); MORTLAKE TAPESTRY. ST JOHN'S COLLEGE

The tapestry works at Mortlake were founded in 1619 with Sir Francis Crane, secretary to Charles I, as controller. The Master Weaver was Philip de Maecht of Brussels. Crane died in 1636 and the following year the king took over the factory. It is possible from St John's College's possession of the tapestry of the *Supper at Emmaus* (c. 1635) that Archbishop Laud was also interested in the Mortlake factory. The subject is based on the painting by Titian which Charles I had purchased from Vincenzo da Gonzaga in 1527 and which is now in the Louvre. The tapestry hangs over the main staircase in the President's Lodgings, and another version is in St George's Chapel, Windsor.

46 ILLUSTRATIONS TO THE OLD AND NEW TESTAMENTS; STAINED-GLASS BY BERNARD VAN LINGE. LINCOLN COLLEGE CHAPEL

The painted glass in the last window of Lincoln College Chapel, dated 1631, is by Bernard van Linge, possibly the brother of Abraham who worked at University College. The subjects are arranged with the types from the Old Testament below and the antitypes from the New Testament above. Each episode in the Life of Christ has its prophetic parallel in the Old Testament; the Last Supper in the Passover; the Crucifixion in the Brazen Serpent and the Resurrection in Jonah disgorged by the Whale. The last mentioned subject also appears in the series in University College Chapel; here the whale is painted a noble shade of purple. The other windows in the chapel are also consistently filled by Van Linge. On the south side are the twelve apostles, dated 1629 and 1630, and on the north twelve prophets from the Old Testament. Other college chapels still containing windows by the van Linges are Balliol, Oriel, Queen's and Wadham.

47 STATUE OF THE VIRGIN AND CHILD ON THE SOUTH PORCH OF THE CHURCH OF ST MARY THE VIRGIN

The south porch of the University Church of St Mary the Virgin was built in 1637 at the expense of the chaplain of Archbishop Laud, Dr Morgan Owen. It has been attributed to Nicholas Stone (1583–1647), who was responsible for the Lyttelton monument in Magdalen College and who designed and built the gateway of the Botanic Garden in 1632. Laud himself said it was the work of a Mr Bromfield. The carver was John Jackson who also worked on Laud's Canterbury Quadrangle at St John's. The porch is markedly Baroque (in the broken pediment and the heavy volutes for instance), unusual not only in Oxford but elsewhere in England at that time. The salomonic pillars were a novel decorative feature. At Ham House a fireplace (c. 1637) with twisted pillars wreathed with vines has been reasonably linked to the cartoon by Raphael of the *Healing of Elymas*, one of the cartoons purchased by Charles I in Genoa in 1623 and used at the Mortlake tapestry works. The pillars of the porch may derive from the same source. In 1905 the porch was wreathed in creeper, which is curious in view of the description of Oxford rising 'from groves which hid all buildings but such as are consecrated to some wise and holy purpose'.

48 THE DOME OF THE RADCLIFFE CAMERA AND THE TOWERS OF ALL SOULS COLLEGE

The view looking West from the upstairs Senior Common Room of Queen's College contains one of the loveliest silhouettes in Oxford. In the centre of the town the stone towers of the North Quadrangle of All Souls constantly catch the eye. On the 12 March 1716 the contract for the south tower to be built according to the design by Nicholas Hawksmoor (1661–1736) was signed by William Townesend (c. 1668–1739). The north tower was begun in 1720. The towers and the adjacent lodgings were financed by three benefactors, one of whom, Philip, first Duke of Wharton, gave his name to the Common Room. The medieval inspiration for the Gothic towers may be found in the west front of Beverley Minster and in the octagon of Ely Cathedral. The Radcliffe Camera was completed under the direction of James Gibbs (1682–1754) in 1749, when the architect received the degree of Honorary M.A.. The Camera is thus the latest addition to Radcliffe Square. It forms the centrepiece of a square which many consider to be one of the most beautiful in Europe.

49 CUPOLA OVER THE GATEWAY. THE QUEEN'S COLLEGE

The cupola over the entrance gate to Queen's College crowns the rusticated screen which links the two wings of the quadrangle. The screen, which was designed by Hawksmoor and modified by Townesend, was built between 1733 and 1736. Occupying the cupola is the statue of 1733 of Queen Caroline by Sir Henry Cheere (1703–81). The following year Cheere contracted to make, for £135 each, three statues of Law, Physic and Poetry for the college. Again in 1737–8 the accounts of the Vice-Chancellor record payment to the sculptor for two statues 'for the theatre'.

The grandiose façade of Queen's, fronting onto the High Street, makes it the more regrettable that nothing ever came of Hawksmoor's ambitious, even glorious, plans for Brasenose of 1734 or of his equally ambitious, if less detailed, ideas for Magdalen in 1724. The front quadrangle of Queen's follows the prototype of the three-sided quadrangle with the fourth side either open to gardens as in Wren's north quadrangle for Trinity College (1668, 1682 and 1728) or closed simply by a single storied screen as here and at All Souls.

50 THREE POUND PIECE AND CROWN OF CHARLES I, MINTED IN OXFORD. HEBERDEN COIN ROOM, ASHMOLEAN MUSEUM

The two coins reproduced, from the mint set up by Charles I at Oxford, are from top to bottom, the obverse and the reverse of the gold three pound piece (1643), probably the finest specimen now surviving, in which the king is represented holding both sword and olive branch, and the obverse of the silver crown of 1644. Like the silver pound, these two coins were designed by Thomas Rawlins and show the influence of Nicholas Briot (active in England from 1625 until his death in 1646). Briot contrived to visit the royal mint at Oxford although still employed in the mint at the Tower of London which was held by the Parliamentary forces. Beneath the equestrian portrait on the silver crown can be seen the city, clearly inscribed *Oxon*. The view is probably taken from Marston. The tower of Magdalen College is discernible under the horse's raised leg; the city walls, bastions and a row of palisades are depicted in the centre.

Thomas Bushell had been authorised to set up a mint for Welsh silver at Aberystwyth in 1637 (hence the device of the Prince of Wales' feathers retained on the three pound piece). In 1642 he was ordered to move to Shrewsbury and then once more to Oxford where the king set up his headquarters in December 1642. The mint was active until the surrender of Oxford in June 1646.

The coins are reproduced a third to a half larger than their actual size.

51 CORONATION CUP OF CHARLES II. TOWN HALL

The collection of plate owned by the City of Oxford, and therefore separate from the University, is now shown in the vaulted crypt of the Town Hall. The Mayors of Oxford shared with the Lord Mayors of London the right to assist the King's butler at the Coronation. Such an occasion is recorded on the silver gilt cup: Donum Regale, Domini Nostri Caroli secundi DG Angliae etc Regis Augustissimi Coronationis festo in Botelaria servienti Sampsoni White, Militi Civitatis Oxonford Majori subdito flagrante rebellione fidelissimo.' The Coronation of Charles II was 'happily celebrated' on St George's

Day 1661. An equally imposing silver gilt cup marks the Coronation of George IV and is inscribed to 'Herberto Parsons'.

52 TOM TOWER. CHRIST CHURCH

The entrance gate of Christ Church had been left incomplete until, in 1681 and 1682, Tom Tower was successfully imposed on the existing buildings by Sir Christopher Wren.

The bell, Great Tom, which has given its name to both tower and quadrangle, was recast by Christopher Hodson in 1680 and must then have weighed over seven tons. Wren's mason, Christopher Kempster, and his assistant, were paid £50 for hoisting it into the tower. It was first officially rung on 29 May 1684 in commemoration of the anniversary of the Restoration. It is also struck every night of the year, one hundred and one times at 9.5 p.m.; the number of strokes denoting the hundred original students of Henry VIII's foundation and the one established by a bequest of 1663.

Christ Church thus benefited from the downfall of Oseney Abbey of the Austin Canons since Tom was one 'of a praiseworthy company/ Douce, Clement, Austin, Hautector, John, Gabriel, Thomas/ once the abbey bells of Oseney'. Of those who have lamented the destruction of the abbey not even Dr Johnson put it as forcefully as Dr Dearmer in 1897: 'as the train moves into Oxford railway station, the stranger may remember that the present approach to the old city is only so hideous because the glorious old abbey has given place to a collection of gasholders, coal-heaps, railway-sidings, modern tomb-stones, and obscene jerry-buildings.' The passage of seventy years has done nothing to alleviate this disgrace.

53 SIR CHRISTOPHER WREN BY EDWARD PIERCE. ASHMOLEAN MUSEUM

The marble bust of Sir Christopher Wren (1632–1723) by Edward Pierce (c. 1635–95) was given to the University by Mr Christopher Wren, son of the sitter, in 1737. Made in 1673, it may have been intended as a present to Wren on the occasion of his knighthood. As mathematician, astronomer, architect and courtier, the place of Wren in the England of the Restoration may be compared with that of Bernini in Rome during and after the pontificate of the Barberini Pope, Urban VIII. Indeed, the echo of Bernini's busts on that of Wren may be due to the latter's knowledge of Bernini's bust of Louis XIV, which he saw on his visit to France in 1665 (notably perhaps in the drilling and modelling of the hair). Sensitive and serene, this has been described by Dr Margaret Whinney as 'the most memorable of all portraits of Wren'. A comparable plaster bust is in All Souls.

54 INTERIOR OF TRINITY COLLEGE CHAPEL

Sir Christopher Wren's frequently quoted remarks made in a letter of 2 March 1692 to the President of Trinity, Dr Bathurst, about the College Chapel (1691–4) demonstrate his own good sense as well as his qualified approbation of the building: 'I considered the design you sent me of your chapel which in the maine is very well, and I believe your work is too far advanced to admit of any advice; however, I have sent my thoughts, which will be of use to the mason to form his mouldings.' Dean Aldrich was, like Wren, also consulted on the subject of the chapel by his friend Dr Bathurst and has been said to have been responsible for its design. The decoration of the interior is perhaps as lavish as is compatible with a Protestant chapel.

55 DETAIL FROM THE CARVING OF THE REREDOS BY GRINLING GIBBONS. TRINITY COLLEGE CHAPEL

Four craftsmen are now thought to have had a hand in the wood-carving in Trinity College Chapel; Arthur Frogley, an Oxford joiner-carver, Jonathan Maine (who was paid £5.8.s), J.van der Stein, who may have carved the sibyls at each end, and Grinling Gibbons. The work of the last named is referred to in 1694–5 by Celia Fiennes in *Journeys through England*, where she mentions the 'beautiful magnificent Structure' with its 'very fine Carving of thin white wood, just like that at Windsor, it being the same hand. [Gibbons presented his and Henry Philips' account for work for

Charles II at Windsor in 1677.] The whole Chappel is wanscoated with Walnut-tree and the fine sweet wood, the same which that the Lord Orfford brought over when High Admiral of England and has wanscoated his hall and staircase with, it is sweet like Cedar and of a reddish collour, but the grain much finer and well vein'd.' The exquisite quality of the carving above the altar, with the dexterous contrast of the colour of the wood used with that of the background, can only be the work of Grinling Gibbons himself (1648–1721).

56 ELIAS ASHMOLE BY JOHN RILEY; THE FRAME BY GRINLING GIBBONS. ASHMOLEAN MUSEUM

In his diary for 2 February 1683 Elias Ashmole (1617–92) refers to a sitting for 'my picture (after sent to Oxford)'. The formal presentation portrait, suitably embellished with a richly carved frame by Grinling Gibbons was painted by John Riley (1646–91) and it was given to the University to mark the foundation of the museum which bears Ashmole's name. This, the oldest museum in Great Britain, was built in Broad Street to house the collections of Ashmole and the Tradescant family; the negotiations for their transfer commenced in 1675, the building was begun in 1679 and the Museum was opened by the Duke of York in 1683. Antiquary, author, alchemist and collector, Ashmole was appointed Windsor Herald by Charles II at the Restoration and published *The institution, laws & ceremonies of the most noble Order of the Garter* in 1672. A copy of this 'unrivalled *locus classicus*' stands beneath Ashmole's right hand. After his retirement from the College of Arms, and his profitable comptrollership of the Excise Office in 1675, Ashmole lived in the house he had acquired in South Lambeth next to the Tradescant's property. Another, less formal, portrait by Riley, that of *Elias Ashmole in Old Age* painted in 1681, is also in the Ashmolean Museum.

57 EAST ENTRANCE OF THE OLD ASHMOLEAN MUSEUM

The East entrance facing the Sheldonian Theatre was not originally intended to be the museum's main entrance, although from 1864 to 1957 it fulfilled that function. In the latter year the main staircase onto Broad Street which had been taken down shortly before 1864, was replaced through the munificence of Mr J.A.Billmeir. This act of generosity marked Mr Billmeir's presentation of a remarkable group of early scientific instruments.

C.H.Josten wrote, in the Tercentenary Number of *Notes and Records of the Royal Society of London*, 'In accordance with the statutes, which Ashmole had formulated himself, the original Ashmolean Museum was primarily a scientific institution ... The museum proper was on the first floor, a large lecture room, called *Schola Naturalis Historiae*, on the ground floor and a chemical laboratory, the first chemical laboratory in the University, in the vaulted basement.' Ashmole was one of the founder members of the Royal Society who agreed to 'meet together weekely (if not hindered by necessary occasions) to consult & debate, concerning the promotion of Experimental learning'. (See also note 56.)

58 MODEL FOR THE DOME OF THE RADCLIFFE CAMERA. 18, ST GILES

At the far end of the garden of 18, St Giles (see also no. 61) underneath a well-established chestnut tree stands a small pedimented pavilion. Supported by four Corinthian pillars it is surmounted by an original model for the dome of the Radcliffe Camera. Another model for the Camera was also put to practical use by following generations. The wooden model (no. 60), having been used as a doll's house by the Dillon children at Ditchley Park, was given to the Bodleian Library by Viscount Dillon in 1913.

59 A VIEW OF THE THEATRE, PRINTING HOUSE, &c.; HEAD-PIECE FOR THE OXFORD ALMANACK OF 1800

This view was drawn by Edward Dayes A.R.A. (1763–1804) and engraved by J.Basire. The buildings, seen from left to right, are the Clarendon Building (1712–5) by Nicholas Hawksmoor, the Sheldonian Theatre (1664–9) named after the Chancellor of the University, Archbishop Gilbert Sheldon, by Sir Christopher Wren and the Old Ashmolean Museum (1679–83), now the Museum of the

History of Science, built in all probability by the master mason Thomas Wood (*c*. 1645–95). Of particular interest are the upright oeil-de-boeuf dormer windows and the lantern of the Sheldonian Theatre shown in the engraving as they were designed by Wren. In 1838 Edward Blore (1787–1879) rebuilt the cupola, which has again been altered, and the dormers were swept away.

The Clarendon Building was originally built to house the University Press. The foundation stone was laid in 1712 and the building was completed in the following year to Hawksmoor's designs and by the work of the mason William Townesend. The statues of the muses on the pediments of the roof were designed by Sir James Thornhill (1675–1734).

60 HAWKSMOOR'S MODEL FOR THE RADCLIFFE CAMERA. BODLEIAN LIBRARY

The history of the building of the Radcliffe Camera is complex. Dr John Radcliffe, Physician to Queen Anne, had decided to contribute towards a new Library for the University in 1712. At first it was intended to attach the new Library to the Selden end of the Bodleian on a site in the grounds of Exeter College, and Hawksmoor's drawings for such a building survive. Radcliffe, however, died in 1714 and directed in his will that the site of the centre of what is now Radcliffe Square should be used. The protracted purchase of the tenements that occupied the position began in 1716. In 1720, Radcliffe's trustees, none of whom were to see the completed library, approached several architects for designs, among them Wren, Vanbrugh, Thornhill, Hawksmoor and Gibbs. As usual Hawksmoor made a number of alternative designs and when negotiations for the site were reopened in 1733 he submitted this elaborately finished model. This was probably made by John Smallwell junior (fl. 1718–61) between 1734 and 1735 when he was paid £87.11.0. for a model. It is of considerable interest that, although it has a square basement and looks back to the great model for Wren's St Paul's, the drum and cupola inspired the finished building, the circular library designed by James Gibbs and built between 1737 and 1749. (See also no. 58.)

61 OVERDOOR ON THE GARDEN FRONT OF 18, ST GILES

The carved overdoor adorns the garden facade of No. 18, St Giles. The house, which belongs to St John's College, formerly served as the Judge's Lodgings until its use reverted to the college in 1966. It was built for Thomas and Elizabeth Rowney in 1702, almost certainly by Bartholomew Peisley II (*c*. 1654–1715). His father, Bartholomew I, had built for St John's the Senior Common Room (1673–6), where an unusual stucco ceiling decorated with shells was added by Thomas Roberts several decades later. For three generations the Peisley family worked as stonemasons and builders in Oxford. Bartholomew Peisley III (*c*. 1683–1727) worked with William Townesend at All Souls and University College (see no. 67).

It was in this house, at one period the town house of the Duke of Marlborough, that the architect Philip Webb (1831–1915), who was born in Beaumont Street, spent his youth. Webb was later to build the Red House at Bexley for William Morris.

62 INTERIOR OF QUEEN'S COLLEGE LIBRARY

It has been suggested by W.G. Hiscock, that the library of Queen's College (1693–4) may have been designed by Henry Aldrich (1648–1710), Dean of Christ Church from 1698 until his death and the architect of Peckwater Quadrangle at Christ Church, built between 1706 and 1714. The finely-carved ends of the book-cases were probably done by the joiner-carver Thomas Minn the Younger. J. van der Stein was paid for cutting eight keystones and two eagles and is thought also to have been responsible for carving the doors of the cupboards at the south end of the library. The pierced work and modelling of these doors, with their deep relief and the felicity of the fruit motifs, approach the virtuosity seen in the carving of Grinling Gibbons. The whole room is united, with a characteristic lightness of touch, by the stucco ceiling added several decades later (in 1756) by Thomas Roberts. It was Roberts who added 'new Ornaments in the Oval Space in the Middle, and the Compartments at the Ends'.

63 CEILING OF THE BUTTERY. ALL SOULS COLLEGE

The buttery of All Souls was probably built at the same time as the hall (1730–3) on which Hawksmoor and Townesend collaborated. Used by the Fellows for luncheon, the furnishings fit its oval shape. The chief glory of this charming room is its ceiling, unique in Oxford, which, like Bernini's church of Sant' Andrea al Quirinale in Rome, demonstrates the grace of an oval design. The bust standing in the alcove is the only known portrait of Hawksmoor, and shows him at the end of his life. Made of plaster painted black to simulate bronze, it was no doubt modelled by Sir Henry Cheere who worked at All Souls in 1732. An interesting possibility is that Roubiliac, who was working in Cheere's workshop at the time, may have had a hand in the bust.

64 GEORGE FREDERICK HANDEL BY LOUIS-FRANCOIS ROUBILIAC. ASHMOLEAN MUSEUM

George Frederick Handel (1685–1759) visited Oxford at the invitation of the Vice-Chancellor, Dr William Holmes, in July 1733 and on 10 July *Athaliah* was given its first performance in the town. The terracotta model by Louis-François Roubiliac (*c*. 1702–62) is for the monument erected to Handel in Westminster Abbey in 1761. It was presented to the University by Mr James Wyatt in 1848. In the completed monument the sheets which are held by Handel's right hand are inscribed with the opening word from the aria in the *Messiah*: 'I know that my Redeemer liveth'. Roubiliac had earlier worked on another statue of Handel, commissioned in 1737 for Vauxhall Gardens and now in the Victoria and Albert Museum. The terracotta model for this is now in the Fitzwilliam Museum, Cambridge. Roubiliac's first important commission in England, and his last, were both of the same sitter, the composer who had also made his home in England.

65 GATES OF THE CLARENDON BUILDING BY JEAN TIJOU

The wrought-iron gates of the Clarendon Building are considered to have been made *c*. 1710 to the designs of Jean Tijou. Although their full beauty in silhouette cannot now be appreciated since it is marred by the addition of two letter boxes, the 'ceremonious richness' of these gates becomes a building in which the administration of the University is now centred and where the Vice-Chancellor and the Hebdomadal Council meet. Tijou's work 'with its wealth of flamboyant repoussé design, the magnificence of which is unequalled in this country' may be compared with the garden gates of New College by Thomas Robinson (1711), which once formed the entrance to a topiary garden, and the gate at All Souls facing onto Catte Street, made to Hawksmoor's designs of 1734.

66 STAIRCASE IN THE RADCLIFFE CAMERA

For 'Plaisterers Work done for the Honble. Trustees at Dr Radcliffe's Library. Per Charles Stanley & Thos. Roberts. To eight ceilings including Grand Stair Case, Coves, and Entablature round, Ornamented with Stucco according to a drawing made by Mr Gibbs at 35£ each as per agreement' £280 was charged, the payment for which was acknowledged by Charles Stanley on 5 March 1744. Gibbs also made the drawings for the 'Rail for the Great Staircase' which Thomas Wagg contracted to make 'in the best manner and of the best Swedish iron' in April 1746. In an estimate of the cost of completing the works on the Libary, which Gibbs submitted to the Trustees in July 1746, £168.10.0 was allowed for 'the Iron Work for the Great Stairs'.

67 DR RADCLIFFE BY FRANCIS BIRD. UNIVERSITY COLLEGE

Dr John Radcliffe was born in 1650 and went up to University College at the age of fifteen. He was awarded a Senior Scholarship and went to Lincoln College as a Fellow taking up his practice in Oxford. In 1684 he moved to London where he was called in by William III and generously fee'd. He built up a large practice and began his benefactions to his former college in the 1690s. Radcliffe died in 1714 and was described as 'an acute observer of symptoms and in many cases peculiarly happy in the treatment of disease'. St Bartholomew's Hospital benefited under the terms of his will and

Oxford can show the Radcliffe Infirmary, the Radcliffe Observatory, the Radcliffe Camera (which housed the Radcliffe Science Library until it was moved in 1866) and the Radcliffe Quadrangle of University College. It is onto this quadrangle that the lead statue of Dr Radcliffe of 1717 by Francis Bird (1667–1731) faces. The quadrangle itself, particularly in the fan-vaulting of the entrance, was built in a traditional Gothic style by Bartholomew Peisley II and William Townesend. It is therefore in contrast to the latter's work for and with Dr Clarke and Hawksmoor.

68 CHRISTOPHER CODRINGTON BY HENRY CHEERE. ALL SOULS COLLEGE LIBRARY

The statue by Sir Henry Cheere of Christopher Codrington stands in the centre of the library. The inscription is dated 1734. Codrington (1668–1710) became a Gentleman Commoner at Christ Church in 1685 and a Fellow of All Souls five years later. 'An accomplished well-bred gentleman, and an universal scholar', he succeeded his father as Captain General of the Leeward Islands and died on his estates in Barbados. He bequeathed £10,000 to All Souls, £6,000 being for the building of the library and the remainder for the purchase of books. He also endowed Codrington College which was built in Barbados between 1714 and 1742. It was not until 1715 that the Warden and Fellows agreed to the building of the library according to Hawksmoor's 'monastick' Gothick designs. Two inspectors were appointed, Dr George Clarke (1661–1736), who had been active in new building schemes for the college since 1703, and Sir Nathaniel Lloyd. Indeed, Dr Clarke was probably responsible for bringing in Hawksmoor. Clarke's large collection of architectural drawings includes numerous designs for All Souls by Hawksmoor, among them one for a roof truss of the Library dated 1716. By 1721 the library was structurally complete. Like the interiors of Hawksmoor's other Gothic buildings that of the library is classical. It is not, however, as originally designed, the stucco ceiling having been completed after Hawksmoor's death by Thomas Roberts of Oxford in 1750.

69 SECOND QUADRANGLE. ORIEL COLLEGE

Unlike the libraries of Queen's College and Christ Church and the Radcliffe Camera, the lower storey of the library designed and built by James Wyatt (1746–1813) for Oriel College was enclosed from the first. The ground floor provided two rooms for the Fellows and these remain in use as the Senior Common Room. The Library above, which houses Lord Leigh's library, has a bay at the east end framed by a pair of green scagliola columns. It was completed in 1788–9. Besides his work on the Radcliffe Observatory (no. 75), Wyatt also remodelled the interiors of Brasenose College Library and the Music School in 1780.

To the left of this second quadrangle of Oriel College is the Carter building of 1729. It balances the Robinson building on the right built by William Townesend in 1719 to 1720. Built in a style 'answerable to the rest of the college' the Carter building shares the high pitched eaves built by Townesend to match those in the front quadrangle. The library was built close up to the buildings of St Mary's Hall, which was reunited to the college in 1902.

70 LIBRARY OF THE MUSEUM OF THE HISTORY OF SCIENCE

The eighteenth-century bookcase which now forms the centrepiece of the Library in the basement of the Museum of the History of Science was formerly in the Picture Gallery of the Bodleian Library. The coat-of-arms of Elias Ashmole was added to the original rocaille cartouche in 1951. On the refectory table in the foreground is an Italian armillary sphere which was acquired for the Lewis Evans collection by purchase in 1952. It is signed *Dominicus Sanctes Sanctini F* and can be dated between 1672 and 1684. Made of brass it demonstrates the planetary system of Heracleides of Pontus (fourth century BC).

71 DRAGON AND INFANT SATYR; DETAIL OF STUCCO IN JESUS COLLEGE HALL

It is tempting to attribute the animated stucco reliefs which support the coat-of-arms of Jesus College above the high table in the hall to Thomas Roberts (see no. 72). The motif, repeated on each side, of a dragon held on a rope by an infant satyr has an air of rococo gaiety reminiscent of the work of François Cuvilliés in Munich. The dragons may be seen as a light-hearted reference to the college's Welsh connection. A more sober reminder of this is found in the panels of gryphons carved on the wooden screen at the opposite end of the hall, which date from 1634.

72 DETAIL OF STUCCO IN CHRIST CHURCH LIBRARY

The stucco decoration of the library of Christ Church was undertaken by Thomas Roberts under the supervision of Dr David Gregory, who became Dean in 1756. For the ceiling Roberts received £663, and in 1759 he was paid £260 for the carving, which presumably included the handsome trophies. The library was finally completed in 1772, fifty-five years after it was begun according to the drawings of William Townesend and Dr Clarke.

73 LOUIS DE VISME BY ANTON RAPHAEL MENGS. CHRIST CHURCH HALL

The portrait of Louis de Visme (1720–76, Student of Christ Church, 1748) by Anton Raphael Mengs (1728–79) is the artist's only portrait in Oxford. Amid the riches of the collection in Christ Church Hall, with its numerous paintings by Reynolds, Gainsborough and Romney, that by Mengs stands out by virtue of its neo-classical simplicity. In its environment, the restraint of de Visme's blue coat and breeches, somewhat modified by his flowered waistcoat, is arresting. So, also, are the sitter's pose and even physiognomy, in that both recall the portraits of Charles III of Spain and of his children which were painted by Mengs in Madrid in the 1760s.

In 1769 the Fellows of All Souls commissioned the artist to paint an altarpiece for their chapel, which was installed in 1771. The subject agreed upon was *Noli me Tangere*, and the fee paid three hundred guineas. Greeted with approbation and popularity the altarpiece gradually fell into disfavour and was ousted from its position a hundred years after its installation. In recent years it has been lent for exhibition to the Birmingham City Art Gallery.

74 PROVOST'S LODGINGS. WORCESTER COLLEGE

Inscribed 'West Front of the Provost's Apartment towards the River, designed to conform to the Centre or Library Building', a drawing by Henry Keene (1726–76) is preserved in Worcester College's collection of architectural drawings. The central building referred to contains the chapel and hall, each in a separate wing fronting onto Beaumont Street, and the library over the colonnade on the side of the quadrangle. It was planned by Dr George Clarke with the assistance of Hawksmoor. At Dr Clarke's death in 1736 the north range had not been begun, although his trustees built part of it according to his designs between 1753 and 1759. The final addition, that of the Provost's Lodgings, departs from Dr Clarke's designs and was completed by Keene between 1773 and 1776. The newly refaced lodgings complement the park-like garden and look out onto the lake. Stocked with fish in 1817 and again with 'tench for lake' in 1818 the 'pond', as it has been slightingly described, was apparently made shortly before 1817. From this latter year until 1822 a good deal of planting and laying of turf was done. The Fellows' garden on the north side of the college contains a fine and fructiferous mulberry.

75 RADCLIFFE OBSERVATORY FROM THE SOUTH

The Radcliffe Observatory maintains a dignified independence from its recent neighbours. There are now grounds for hope that the modern, ugly, albeit necessary, additions made on the site will be replaced by lawns and trees similar to those that stood there before the Radcliffe Trustees sold the Observatory, as a result of their decision in 1929 to build another in the purer air of Pretoria in South Africa. It was acquired by Lord Nuffield for £100,000 and half the site was given to the Infirmary.

Initially the plans were those of Henry Keene and work was begun in 1772. The octagonal tower is based on the Temple of the Winds in Athens. John Bacon R.A. (1740–99) carved the Winds at the top of the building and also executed in bronze the figures of Hercules and Atlas who support the globe on the roof. The signs of the Zodiac above the windows on the first floor have been attributed to John Charles Felix Rossi R.A. (1762–1839). In 1773 'another elevation' was adopted, and this is presumed to have been that of James Wyatt, since on Keene's death in 1776 he was entrusted with the completion of the Observatory, which was achieved in 1794.

76 SIR THOMAS LE BRETON BY SIR THOMAS LAWRENCE. PEMBROKE COLLEGE
The portrait of Sir Thomas le Breton (1763–1838), Baili and President of the States of Jersey in 1826, hangs in the Senior Common Room of Pembroke College. Other portraits by Sir Thomas Lawrence P.R.A. (1769–1830) to be found in the colleges, apart from that of the Prince Regent in the Examination Schools, include the portrait of Sir Charles Vaughan in the hall of All Souls and that of the architect John Nash in Jesus College. Lawrence's remarkable collection of drawings by Michelangelo and Raphael are noted below (see no. 85).

77 EAST FRONT OF THE TAYLORIAN INSTITUTION BY CHARLES ROBERT COCKERELL
On 10 June 1839, Dr Philip Bliss as Registrar of the University issued the announcement concerning the requirements for the Taylorian Institute and the Ashmolean Museum: 'It is desirable that, externally, the two buildings should harmonize and, if possible form parts of one architectural design, which is required to be of a Grecian character. The Taylor building to be placed at the eastern end, care being taken that its façade towards St Giles's Street, one of the principal entrances into Oxford, be sufficiently ornamental.' The competition was won by Charles Robert Cockerell R.A. (1788–1863) who, after the death of George Basevi in 1845, assisted in the conclusion of the Fitzwilliam Museum at Cambridge. This period of work in Oxford also included the overweighty design for the lower part of Queen's College Library (1843–5) formerly, like the Radcliffe Camera, an open loggia. The advanced columns of the façade on St Giles bear allegorical figures of France, Italy, Germany and Spain. These may be compared with those of Pitzhanger Manor by Sir John Soane (c. 1802) and those in Cockerell's unaccepted design for the Royal Exchange. Recent cleaning has revealed the architect's skilful and contrasting use of white and honey-coloured stone. One of the last classical buildings in Oxford (1841–5), Cockerell's achievement wins increasingly unanimous praise.

78 FORMERLY CANAL HOUSE, NOW THE MASTER'S LODGINGS. ST PETER'S COLLEGE
Nuffield College is built over the wharfs and quays of the Oxford Canal Company, bought by Lord Nuffield in 1937, which in turn had replaced 'Badcock's Garden' with the coming of the canal to Oxford in 1790. The Canal House, which is now the lodging of the Master of St Peter's College, with its pedimented entrance and pilastered sides, formerly overlooked the New Road basin. Behind it can be seen the regimental brick building that disguises the architectural amalgam which now comprises St Peter's College. The former Wesleyan School, for instance, has been transformed into rooms for undergraduates. To the left of centre is the tower of the church of St Peter le Bailey, now the college chapel. Beyond can be seen the dome of the Radcliffe Camera, and the spires of St Mary's, the University Church, and All Saints, the City Church.

79 GREEN SIBERIAN MARBLE VASE GIVEN BY TSAR ALEXANDER I IN 1816. MERTON COLLEGE CHAPEL
Among the reminders of the visit of the Allied Sovereigns to Oxford in 1814 (which include the portraits of Tsar Alexander I, Frederick Wiliam III, King of Prussia and of the Prince Regent in the Examination Schools), one of the most handsome is tucked away in the north transept of Merton College Chapel. Inscribed on the plinth in Latin and in Russian, the massive vase of green Siberian marble was presented to the college by the Tsar in 1816 in gratitude for the hospitality he had received there. Better suited to a Roman church

or palace, the vase stands unused in all its pristine, highly-polished state.

80 MEMORIAL TO PERCY BYSSHE SHELLEY BY EDWARD ONSLOW FORD. UNIVERSITY COLLEGE
Originally intended for the English Cemetery in Rome, the Shelley Memorial was presented to University College by Lady Shelley, the poet's daughter-in-law, in 1893. Percy Bysshe Shelley (1792–1822) went up in October 1810 as Lord Leicester Scholar. In March the following year he was sent down for 'contumaciously refusing to answer questions proposed to him and for also repeatedly declining to disavow a publication entitled *The Necessity of Atheism*'. Like the memorial to Jowett it was designed by Edward Onslow Ford (1852–1901) and is set in a chamber designed for it by Basil Champneys (1842–1935), the architect who designed the Indian Institute, now threatened with demolition. The figure is carved out of white Carrara marble, while the plinth, on which are the Mourning Muse of Poetry and two gryphons both in bronze, is of veined Connemara marble.

Another association linked to the site on which the memorial to Shelley now stands is recorded by a plaque on the outside wall onto the High Street: 'In a house on this site between 1655 and 1668 lived ROBERT BOYLE. Here he discovered BOYLE'S LAW and made experiments with an AIR PUMP designed by his assistant ROBERT HOOKE Inventor Scientist & Architect who made a MICROSCOPE & thereby first identified the LIVING CELL.'

81 ST IGNATIUS LOYOLA ATTRIBUTED TO JUAN MARTINEZ MONTAÑES. CAMPION HALL
In 1935 Campion Hall moved from St Giles, where it had been since 1896, into buildings designed for it by Sir Edwin Lutyens (1869–1944) between 1934 and 1936. These stand behind Pembroke College in Brewer Street, and enclose the gardens of Micklem Hall. Numerous gifts and purchases were made during the 1930s under the Mastership of Father D'Arcy. Among these is the gilded and painted carving of the founder of the Society of Jesus, St Ignatius Loyola, with his followers, which is attributed to Juan Martinez Montañes of Seville (1568–1649). St Ignatius is represented in a pose recalling that of the Madonna della Miserocordia. The group, which was presented by Maurice Wilkinson and was formerly in the collection of Sir Charles Allom, occupies a dominant position facing the entrance to the dining hall.

82 KEBLE COLLEGE CHAPEL BY WILLIAM BUTTERFIELD
The Chapel dominates Keble quadrangle, as is fitting in a college 'constituted with the especial object and intent of providing persons desirous of academical education and willing to live economically with a college wherein sober living and high culture of the mind may be combined with Christian training based upon the principles of the Church of England'. Such were the terms of the Royal Charter of Incorporation of 1868. The college was built between 1868 and 1882 in variecoloured brick exuberantly diapered. The architect was the 'great exponent of the Gothic Revival', William Butterfield (1814–1900). The just combination of criticism and praise meted out by John Betjeman in *An Oxford University Chest* (1938) can scarcely be bettered: 'It is unfortunate that William Butterfield ... should have paid so little regard to the texture and colour of Oxford stone in this, his largest work in Oxford. As an essay in the right arrangement of masses, in good proportion and originality in the Gothic manner, Keble College is by far the best Gothic Revival work in either Oxford or Cambridge.'

83 VENETIAN WINDOWS BY SIR THOMAS GRAHAM JACKSON, SEEN FROM A WINDOW ON THE HALL STAIRCASE. HERTFORD COLLEGE
The triple Venetian windows (1890) of the north-west range of the main quadrangle of Hertford College are seen from the staircase leading to the hall. Both were designed by Sir Thomas Graham Jackson (1835–1924) who was also responsible for the chapel, the 'Bridge of Sighs' and the College barge between 1887 and 1890 and 1903 and 1908. 'No other man' wrote H.S.Goodhart-Rendel 'has

altered the appearance of Oxford in modern times so greatly as Jackson.' The new buildings at Brasenose and Trinity, the Oxford High School for Boys (1881), and the Examination Schools (1877–82), particularly vast and daunting, are all in the 'Anglo-Jackson' style, a Victorian variant of the Jacobean, which has not yet won many admirers.

84 AN ELDERLY WOMAN WITH CLASPED HANDS BY MATHIS NITHART, CALLED GRÜNEWALD. ASHMOLEAN MUSEUM
The drawing of *An Elderly Woman with Clasped Hands* by Mathis Nithart known as Gothart and more generally Grünewald (*c.* 1478–1528) is the only known drawing by the artist in Britain. Probably a study for the Virgin at the foot of the Cross its documentary interest and importance equals its rarity. Francis Douce, an antiquary and inveterate collector, bequeathed it to the University in 1834. Together with numerous other drawings and prints of the Northern Schools from the Douce Bequest, it was transferred from the Bodleian Library to the Ashmolean Museum in 1863. Born in 1757, and for a time Keeper of the Manuscripts at the British Museum, Douce inherited a legacy from Joseph Nollekens in 1823. His outstanding group of medieval manuscripts, together with the manuscript of his *Diary of Antiquarian Purchases* kept over thirty years, is preserved in the Bodleian Library.

85 BRONZE HEAD OF MICHELANGELO, CAST FROM HIS DEATH MASK, BY DANIELE DA VOLTERRA. ASHMOLEAN MUSEUM
Daniele Ricciarelli da Volterra (1509–66) made a number of casts from the death-mask of Michelangelo (1475–1564). Six in bronze are recorded in the inventory compiled after Daniele's death and it is likely that eight or more were produced and that the bronze head in the Ashmolean Museum is one of these. It was presented to the University in 1845 by William Woodburn and can be regarded as a memorial to the public spiritedness of his brother Samuel, the dealer in drawings. Samuel Woodburn, having helped Sir Thomas Lawrence to build up his collection of old master drawings, endeavoured to preserve it in its entirety after the death of Lawrence in 1830. After many setbacks and further negotiations, the drawings by Michelangelo and Raphael were acquired for the University in 1845 by public subscription. This was largely raised by the initiative of the Revd Dr Henry Wellesley and the munificence of the second Earl of Eldon.

86 TYMPANUM OVER THE ENTRANCE TO 62, BANBURY ROAD
The development of the area of North Oxford, on and surrounding the Banbury Road, began with the Park Town Estate of 1853. The designs for the Norham Manor estate, now endangered by the proposed enlargement of the Pitt Rivers Museum, which was to link the Park Town area and the northern edge of the city, were drawn up by William Wilkinson in 1860. The development occupied the next twenty years. Two other architects who were also engaged in the work were the local Frederick Codd and E. G. Bruton. Bruton's No. 62, Banbury Road (1864) has a remarkable tympanum over the entrance to the front door. It is carved in relief, possibly to the design of John Hungerford Pollen and is inscribed, somewhat inhospitably, 'Things go well in going'. No. 62 now houses the Department of Surveying and Geodesy.

87 CHINOISERIE BRIDGE OVER THE RIVER CHERWELL, FROM ST HILDA'S COLLEGE
The recent Chinoiserie bridge is one of the two which connect the buildings of Magdalen College School with the playing fields on the island in the Cherwell. The river branches here and one part of it forms the western boundary of St Hilda's College, founded by Miss Dorothea Beale, the Principal of Cheltenham Ladies' College, in 1893. Miss Beale bought Cowley House in Cowley Place, with four acres of land for £5,000. The once elegant house built by Dr John Sibthorp is now irreparably encased in the fabric of St Hilda's. However, the college enjoys virtually uninterrupted views across the Cherwell to the Broad Walk in Christ Church Meadow. Perhaps, in years to come, if the University ever becomes fully co-educational,

the charm of the college's riverside position will be realised once more by the removal of the protective fence which runs along the river front.

88 INTERIOR OF THE SCIENCE MUSEUM BY BENJAMIN WOODWARD
The Science Museum designed by Benjamin Woodward (1815–61) was built between 1855 and 1858 in a style designated as 'Veronese Gothic of the best and manliest type in a new and striking combination' and more recently and aptly as 'Venetic Gothic' (see pp. 145 and 150). The view of the interior shows the Gothicised ironwork supporting the roof – 'the difficulty was to do this without limiting the design to the many structural features of the Crystal Palace or condescending to vulgar detail of a railway terminus' wrote Sir Charles Eastlake. The progress of the building was fatally handicapped by lack of funds; the £30,000 voted for the construction covered only the bare structure. Rossetti who expected 'myself to have to do in some way with the decorations as the building goes on', continued 'I believe the interior decoration has to be provided by special subscription.' Ruskin wrote to Dr (later Sir) Henry Acland 'I will pay for a good deal myself, and I doubt not to find funds. *Such* capitals as we will have.' Despite this early optimism the interior has never reached completion and the same fate has befallen the work of the brothers O'Shea on the façade on which the University 'carved … the image of her Parsimony' (Ruskin).

89 BAS-RELIEF FROM THE PALACE OF KING ASHUR-NASIR-PAL, MAGDALEN COLLEGE
The bas-relief of the winged human-headed genie with its hands resting on the stylised 'sacred tree' comes from the palace at Nimrud of the Assyrian King Ashur-nasir-pal (883–859 BC) the son, as the inscription states, of Tukulti-Ninurta (890–884 BC). Similar reliefs in Oxford are in the Ashmolean Museum and at Christ Church, while a bas-relief which probably relates to it is now at Yale University.
In 1842 the British Ambassador to the Porte, Sir Stratford Canning, later Lord Stratford de Redcliffe, met Sir Austen Henry Layard (1817–94) in Istanbul, and in the same year Layard met the young Hormuzd Rassam. In 1845, due to his continued exertions the Ambassador obtained a firman which enabled Layard to begin excavations at Nimrud partially financed by Canning. Rassam, who was born at Mosul in 1826, assisted Layard from 1845 to 1847. For a brief period in 1848 he went to Magdalen College to conclude his studies. Either in this year or in 1849 he gave to the college the bas-relief which is now in the President's Lodgings. Rassam again assisted Layard in 1849 to 1851 and after an adventurous life in British service in Aden and Ethiopia later carried on excavations for the Trustees of the British Museum at Nineveh and Nimrud every year from 1876 to 1882. He died in 1910.

90 MEMORIAL TO BENJAMIN JOWETT BY EDWARD ONSLOW FORD. BALLIOL COLLEGE CHAPEL
The memorial to Benjamin Jowett (1817–93; Master of Balliol College from 1870 until his death) was designed and made in 1894 by Edward Onslow Ford. M. H. Spielmann described it in 1901 as 'a very beautiful composition full of colours, with its mosaics, its figures light and dark, its armorial bearings, its marbles, its metals and its lettering decoration in its widest meaning being here wedded to sculpture for the achievement of a pleasing result.' It is startling to realise that all these varied materials are combined in a diminutive monument, scarcely more than three feet square, which aptly echoes Jowett's own slight stature. However, the memorial, with its sarcophagus recalling that by Alfred Stevens for the Duke of Wellington's monument in St Paul's Cathedral, is 'essentially joyous symbolising happiness and pride in the man'.

91 MAX BEERBOHM, THE ENCAENIA OF 1908. ASHMOLEAN MUSEUM
The Encaenia of 1908 by Sir Max Beerbohm (1872–1956, Merton College 1890–4) is a characteristically delicately coloured caricature

of the newly installed Chancellor of the University, Lord Curzon 'being an humble hint … based on the Encaenia of 1907, whereby so many idols of the market-place were cheerily set up in the groves of the Benign Mother.' Among the 'idols' thus wittily suggested as unsuitable recipients of honorary degrees at the annual Encaenia held in June may be identified (from left to right) Sir Arthur Conan Doyle, Eugene Sandow (a circus weight-lifter), the Prince of Wales (then aged fourteen; he was at Magdalen College from 1912–14 and was 'set up' as D.C.L. in 1915), Little Tich (Harry Relph, the actor and comic vocalist) and John Burns (the first Labour President of the Board of Trade).

92 THE STRUCTURE OF VITAMIN B₁₂, DISCOVERED AT OXFORD

Many important scientific developments have been made in Oxford in the twentieth century; of particular note are the work on atomic numbers by H. G.-J. Moseley, who was killed at Gallipoli in 1915, Florey and Chain's work on penicillin, and, more recently, work by Dr Dorothy Hodgkin and her colleagues in X-ray crystallography. The diagram illustrates the evidence obtained by them through X-ray analysis of the chemical structure of vitamin B_{12}.

Red crystals of the vitamin were first isolated from liver as a factor active against pernicious anaemia and sent for examination to Oxford in 1948. Study of the diffraction effects observed when X-rays were passed through the crystals made it possible to calculate a map in three dimensions of the electron density in the crystals. Peaks of electron density, contoured at intervals of 1 electron per cubic Ångstrøm, mark the relative positions of the atoms in space, and hence, in outline, the way in which they are chemically linked to one another. The heavy atom in the centre of the molecule is cobalt.

93 STATUE OF ST JOHN THE BAPTIST BY ERIC GILL ON THE TOWER OF ST JOHN'S COLLEGE

The statue of St John the Baptist on the east side of the tower over the entrance gate of St John's college is by Eric Gill (1882–1940). Two statues were commissioned from the sculptor by Sir Edward Maufe, the second being for Guildford Cathedral, of which the donor was the architect. The figure was unveiled in 1935. It occupies the niche in the fifteenth-century tower of the Cistercian St Bernard's College, which was founded by Henry Chichele, Archbishop of Canterbury, in 1437. The college of St John the Baptist, founded by Sir Thomas White in 1557, occupied the site and the buildings of Chichele's foundation.

94 BRONZE FOUNTAIN BY HUBERT DALWOOD. NUFFIELD COLLEGE

The bronze fountain which confronts the visitor entering the quadrangle of Nuffield College occupies an axial position. The first fountain undertaken by the sculptor Hubert Dalwood, and completed in 1962, it demanded ingenuity in the direction of the flow of water and in maintaining the equal strength of the flow. The compositon suggests an inverted helmet and a shield. In commissioning the fountain the senior members of the college followed their chosen principle of employing contemporary artists for the decoration and embellishment of Lord Nuffield's foundation. John Piper was similarly engaged in the design of the chapel and the stained glass windows. While it may appear paradoxical to combine this laudable practice with the building of the college in a quasi-traditional style, which was energetically criticised both during its construction and after its completion in 1958, the result is not unsuccessful.

95 PROPOSED NEW BUILDING BY POWELL AND MOYA. CHRIST CHURCH

Detail of the east elevation of staircase 1 in the proposed new building. The plans were drawn up by Powell and Moya in 1964 and the building, which is at present under construction, will occupy a site in the north-west corner of the college. It will front directly onto Blue Boar Street to the north, while the south elevation will look across the gardens to the north range of Tom Quad.

96 POWELL AND MOYA'S NEW BUILDING. BRASENOSE COLLEGE

One of, if not the most, rewarding new building in Oxford is that built on an extremely limited site for Brasenose College. Designed by Philip Powell and Hidalgo Moya and completed in 1961, it brilliantly replaced lavatories and bicycle sheds with a modern building which is in harmony with its neighbours. While its position makes it difficult to see, or to comprehend, as a whole, grandeur is achieved in the severely restricted space. A fellow-architect has described it as 'one of the loveliest small buildings I know'. Thirty-two rooms were created for undergraduates. The *Reclining Figure* in the foreground is by Henry Moore and is lent the college by Mrs Irina Moore.

97 LAW LIBRARY BY SIR LESLIE MARTIN AND C. ST J. WILSON

The Law Library, effectively dominating the site on Manor Road, where it replaces the former Territorial Army Drill Hall, also houses the English Faculty Library, a library for the Institute of Statistics, and the Gulbenkian Lecture Theatre. Designed by Professor Sir Leslie Martin and C. St John Wilson, the building, for which the Rockefeller Foundation made a grant of £150,000 was begun in 1959. On 17 October 1964 it was opened by Dr Erwin N. Griswold, Dean of the Harvard Law School. The building combines massiveness with a soaring, or floating quality. The frame of the building is of reinforced concrete 'clad externally with brickwork, selected to harmonize with the stonework used in the locality'.

98 DETAIL OF THE WOLFSON BUILDING. ST ANNE'S COLLEGE

The Wolfson building, designed by Howell, Killick, Partridge and Amis for St Anne's College, and built by Hinkins and Frewin, was opened in 1964. The other existing buildings, Hartland House (1938) by Sir Giles Gilbert Scott O.M. (1880–1960) and the college hall (1959) by Gerald Banks are ultimately to be linked by an open cloister. This will run through the first, Wolfson, building and the other five buildings which are designed to 'form a sweeping curved line on the east and south of the site', and so 'will create a freely shaped enclosure round the present college lawn'. The proposed plan is novel and interesting as it is intended to provide a covered way which will reach all parts of the college. It represents, once again, an application of the idea of a colonnade or piazza of the eighteenth century and of the earlier cloister to contemporary buildings.

99 RIVER BUILDING BY ARNE JACOBSEN. ST CATHERINE'S COLLEGE

The view of St Catherine's College is of the River Building and the Water Garden facing west from the site near the River Cherwell in Holywell Great Meadow. The foundation stone was laid in 1960 and the buildings were virtually complete at the time of the official opening on October 16 1964. The total cost, including the endowment of the college, has been put at £2,750,000. The Danish architect, Arne Jacobsen, received the commission which extended to every detail, chairs, tables, cutlery and light fittings. The result is consistent to an unusual degree. It will be for a later generation to judge whether or not such a consistency triumphs over a certain rigidity in the design as well as an horizontal emphasis which is foreign to a city where the eye is constantly drawn upwards.

100 THE NEW ENGINEERING LABORATORY

The department of Engineering Science was founded in 1907. The new Engineering Laboratory was opened by the Duke of Edinburgh on 15 November 1963 and had been partly occupied in the preceding year. After several months of discussion the original plans for the building by Professor Basil Ward, of Ramsey, Murray, White and Ward, were published in October 1959. Consisting of eight storeys, the laboratory dominates the skyline of Oxford from the North, not only by its height (110 feet), but chiefly by its bulk. Originally ten storeys were planned but the advice of the Royal Fine Art Commission and the City Council was heeded. The wing-shaped roof line is dictated by the unusual top floor. In addition to the library and the lecture rooms, it accommodates a shallow tank of water to provide constant head pressure for the hydraulics laboratory.

Acknowledgments

I am most grateful to Sir Maurice Bowra, not only for his Introduction, but for his advice and encouragement; and to Mr Ian Lowe for his Notes, and guidance on architectural questions.

Dr W. A. Pantin, Keeper of the University Archives, has kindly read my draft chapters and rescued me from many an error.

On particular aspects I have received much valuable help from Dr E. J. Bowen, Sir Wilfred Le Gros Clark, Mr A. C. Crombie, Sir Robert Hall, Principal of Hertford College, Dr R. Highfield, Professor G. Harris, Professor R. V. Jones, Mr T. C. Keeley and Professor H. M. Powell.

I am grateful to Mr Michael Raeburn for his planning and production of the book, and to Mrs Mary Denniston for checking the proofs.

I wish to thank the Provost and Fellows of Oriel College for permission to quote from the Newman–Hawkins correspondence, and the Clarendon Press, Oxford, for permission to quote from *Studies in Medieval Culture* by C. H. Haskins.

Felix Markham

The author, photographer and publishers wish to thank the Heads and Governing Bodies of all the Oxford Colleges, the Lord Mayor of Oxford, and the authorities of the Ashmolean Museum, the Museum of the History of Science and the Bodleian Library, by whose permission photographs of objects in their collections are reproduced. Their unfailing help and generous cooperation has made it possible for many of Oxford's most precious treasures to be illustrated in this book.

They also wish to thank the following for photographs supplied: Ashmolean Museum, plates 7, 59; University Press, plates 9, 13, 60, 73; Museum of the History of Science, plate 92; Messrs Powell and Moya, plate 95; other sources, plates 1–3, 10, 15, 18, 19, 25, 27, 28, 31, 35–8, 40–4, 47–9, 55, 56, 63, 66, 68, 80, 81, 84, 85, 91, 94.

The map of Oxford was drawn by Sidney Woods and is based on maps in *An Inventory of the Historical Monuments in the City of Oxford* (H.M.S.O., 1939), and on information supplied by the Ordnance Survey (Oxford). It is based upon the Ordnance Survey map with the sanction of the Controller of Her Britannic Majesty's Stationery Office, Crown Copyright Reserved.

Information for the note on plate 92 (taken from the *Proceedings of the Royal Society*, 1957, *242A*, 228) was kindly supplied by Dr Dorothy Crowfoot Hodgkin, F.R.S..

Ian Lowe wishes particularly to acknowledge his debt to the published works of H. M. Colvin, Dr Kerry Downes, S. G. Gillam, the late Rupert Gunnis, the late W. G. Hiscock, Oliver Millar, Dr W. A. Pantin, Sir John Summerson and Dr Margaret Whinney.

He wishes to thank Mr John Betjeman for permission to quote from his *Oxford University Chest*, published by John Miles, and the Clarendon Press, Oxford, for permission to quote from the *Victoria History of the County of Oxford*.

Opposite. Map of the central part of the city of Oxford, showing the colleges, permanent private halls, churches, the most important buildings and the old city wall. Lady Margaret Hall, St Anne's, St Antony's and St Hugh's Colleges, and the proposed site of Wolfson College are off the map to the north of the city.

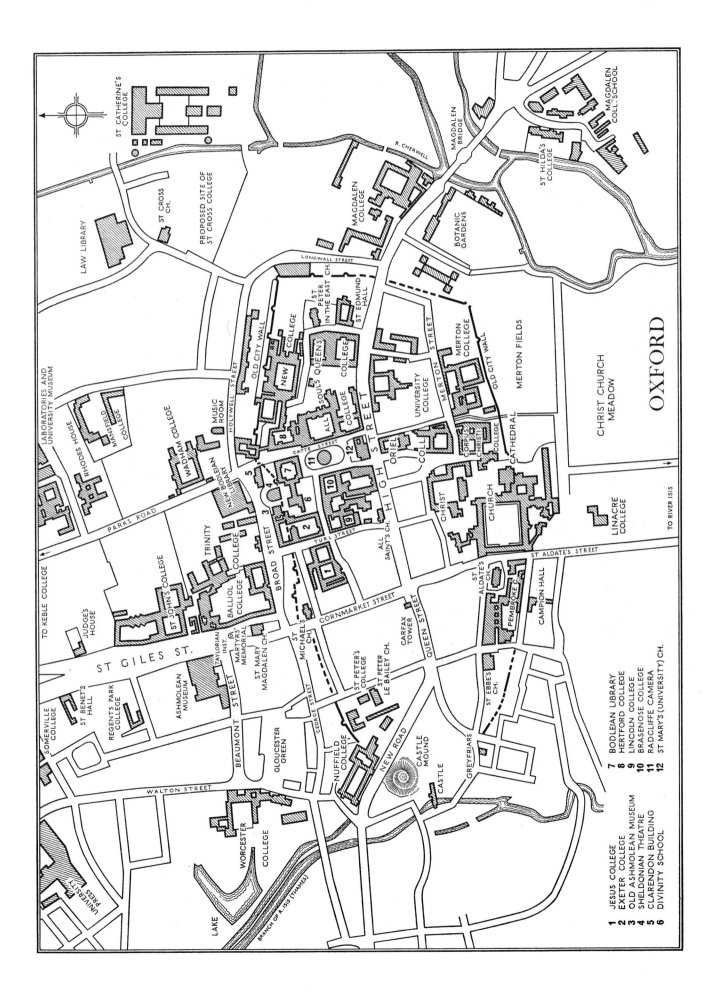

OXFORD

1 JESUS COLLEGE
2 EXETER COLLEGE
3 OLD ASHMOLEAN MUSEUM
4 SHELDONIAN THEATRE
5 CLARENDON BUILDING
6 DIVINITY SCHOOL

7 BODLEIAN LIBRARY
8 HERTFORD COLLEGE
9 LINCOLN COLLEGE
10 BRASENOSE COLLEGE
11 RADCLIFFE CAMERA
12 ST MARY'S (UNIVERSITY) CH.

ST CATHERINE'S COLLEGE
ST CROSS CH.
PROPOSED SITE OF ST CROSS COLLEGE
LAW LIBRARY
R. CHERWELL
MAGDALEN BRIDGE
MAGDALEN COLL. SCHOOL
ST HILDA'S COLLEGE
MAGDALEN COLLEGE
ST PETER IN THE EAST CH.
ST EDMUND HALL
LONGWALL STREET
BOTANIC GARDENS
NEW COLLEGE
OLD CITY WALL
ALL SOULS
QUEEN'S COLLEGE
MERTON STREET
MERTON COLLEGE
MERTON FIELDS
LABORATORIES AND UNIVERSITY MUSEUM
HOLYWELL STREET
CATTE STREET
UNIVERSITY COLLEGE
OLD CITY WALL
CHRIST CHURCH MEADOW
RHODES HOUSE
MANSFIELD COLLEGE
WADHAM COLLEGE
MUSIC ROOM
NEW BODLEIAN LIBRARY
HIGH STREET
ORIEL COLLEGE
CORPUS CHRISTI COLLEGE
CATHEDRAL
LINACRE COLLEGE
PARKS ROAD
TRINITY
BALLIOL COLLEGE
TURL STREET
ALL SAINT'S CH.
CHRIST CHURCH
TO RIVER ISIS
TO KEBLE COLLEGE
ST JOHN'S COLLEGE
BROAD STREET
ST ALDATE'S STREET
JUDGE'S HOUSE
TAYLORIAN INST.
MARTYRS' MEMORIAL
ST MARY MAGDALEN CH.
ST MICHAEL'S CH.
CORNMARKET STREET
CARFAX TOWER
QUEEN STREET
ST ALDATE'S CH.
PEMBROKE C.
CAMPION HALL
ST GILES ST.
ASHMOLEAN MUSEUM
ST PETER'S COLLEGE
ST PETER LE BAILEY CH.
ST EBBE'S CH.
SOMERVILLE COLLEGE
ST BENET'S HALL
REGENTS PARK COLLEGE
BEAUMONT STREET
GLOUCESTER GREEN
GEORGE STREET
NUFFIELD COLLEGE
NEW ROAD
CASTLE MOUND
GREYFRIARS
WALTON STREET
CASTLE
UNIVERSITY PRESS
WORCESTER COLLEGE
LAKE
BRANCH OF R. ISIS (THAMES)

Index